Instructor's Guide to Accompany
CRAFTING A COMPILER

CHARLES N. FISCHER
RICHARD J. LEBLANC, JR.

The Benjamin/Cummings Publishing Company, Inc.
Menlo Park, California • Reading, Massachusetts •
Fort Collins, Colorado • Don Mills, Ontario • Wokingham, U.K. •
Amsterdam • Sydney • Singapore • Tokyo • Madrid • Bogota •
Santiago • San Juan

Acknowledgments

We gratefully acknowledge the contributions of G. A. Venkatesh, Will Winsborough, and Felix Wu, whose careful and elegant solutions were the basis of the solution set presented in this instructor's guide. If the average student were as able as these individuals, teaching would be a great deal easier.

Copyright © 1988 by The Benjamin/Cummings Publishing Company, Inc.

All rights reserved. No part of this publication may be reproduced, stored in a retrieval system, or transmitted in any form or by any means, electronic, mechanical, photocopying, recording, or otherwise, without prior written permission of the publisher. Printed in the United States of America. Published simultaneously in Canada.

ISBN 0-8053-3202-2

BCDEFGHIJ-DM-9543210

The Benjamin/Cummings Publishing Company, Inc.
2727 Sand Hill Road
Menlo Park, CA 94025

Table of Contents

1. Introduction 1

2. Choice Of Project Implementation Language 1

3. Sample Outlines 2

3.1. Senior-Level 10 Week Introductory Course 2

3.2. Senior-Level 14 Week Introductory Course 3

3.3. Graduate-Level 14 Week Course 3

4. Project Software 4

5. Project Suggestions 7

5.1. A Simple Project 7

5.2. An Intermediate Project (Macro) 8

5.3. A Challenging Project (Ada/CS) 8

6. Selected Solutions 13

6.1. Chapter 3 Solutions 13

6.2. Chapter 4 Solutions 26

6.3. Chapter 5 Solutions 30

6.4. Chapter 6 Solutions 40

6.5. Chapter 7 Solutions 50

6.6. Chapter 8 Solutions 55

6.7. Chapter 9 Solutions 63

6.8. Chapter 10 Solutions 72

6.9. Chapter 11 Solutions 79

6.10. Chapter 12 Solutions 90

6.11. Chapter 13 Solutions 103

6.12. Chapter 14 Solutions 108

6.13. Chapter 15 Solutions 109

6.14. Chapter 16 Solutions 121

6.15. Chapter 17 Solutions 130

1. Introduction

Crafting a Compiler presents a practical approach to the subject of compiler construction, based on the experience of the authors as compiler implementors and as developers of compiler construction courses. It is intended to provide the reader not only with a good understanding of all of the components of a compiler, but also with a real sense of how they actually fit together to make a working, usable compiler. We believe that this philosophy is a distinguishing feature of the book. Since we are concerned with presenting the most modern compiler construction techniques, we emphasize the use of compiler tools to generate the components, wherever practical. Source code for the tools described in Appendices B through F of the text is available from the publisher; contact your Addison Wesley/Benjamin Cummings sales representative for details.

As a classroom text, *Crafting a Compiler* is oriented toward a particular course organization that we have developed over the last twelve years. This course organization and the book are quite flexible, having been used in courses ranging from a three credit senior-level course taught in a ten-week quarter to a six credit semester-long graduate course. (See the sample course outlines below.) A cohesive implementation project is an important part of this course organization and thus the book has a strong practical orientation to support such a project.

Appendix A contains the definition of a language we call Ada/CS, which is principally a substantial subset of the Ada programming language. For pedagogical reasons, it is not a strict subset. Recommended projects for a course using this book involve implementation of some or all of Ada/CS, depending on the length and level of the course and on the amount of time students can be expected to spend working of a project. A selection of possible projects is presented below.

A recursive descent compiler for a very simple subset of Ada/CS is presented and discussed in Chapter 2. Code for a complete working compiler for this subset is included with the tools mentioned above. Making the project an extension of this working compiler enables students to complete a significant project even in a course as short as one quarter. This extension approach is valuable even if limited time is not a factor. Requiring students to read and extend a substantial program provides them with important experience that is not commonly available in many computer science curricula. It also teaches them a great deal about how the pieces of a compiler fit together—something that is hard to teach any other way.

2. Choice Of Project Implementation Language

A secondary purpose for our presentation of Ada/CS in Appendix A is that it can serve as a tutorial on the features of Ada we use as the basis of the pseudocode used in examples throughout the book. It is certainly not necessary that a student be familiar with Ada to use this book. Our pseudocode should be easily understandable to anyone familiar with Pascal or Modula-2, perhaps after a brief study of Appendix A.

Nor is it necessary that any particular language be used to implement the project in a course based on this book. The pseudocode serves perfectly well as a design description, regardless of the chosen implementation language. In addition, the scanner and parser generation tools we provide produce tables, not programs, so they can be used in any language environment. At the time this guide is written, the authors both use Pascal as the implementation language in their courses. Likewise, all of the tools are written in Pascal, as are the starter compilers and the drivers that use tables produced by the scanner and parser generators. Use of the Yacc and Lex generators with C as an implementation language is certainly a viable alternative, as, of course, is use of Ada and Modula-2 along with our generators. In any case, our pseudocode should serve effectively as a sketch of the required implementation.

We base our recommended project and our pseudocode on the Ada language because that language includes virtually all of the features we wished to discuss in our chapters on semantic analysis. Had we chosen any other language as our basis (Modula-2, for example), we would have had to describe a number of extensions in order to discuss techniques for compiling such things as exit statements, exception handling and operator overloading. Thus the comprehensiveness of Ada was the overriding factor in our language decision.

3. Sample Outlines

Following are three sample outlines for introductory compiler courses. All presume that a project will be a major component of the course. All of the outlines include top-down parsing early in the course with coverage of LR parsing deferred to the end. We feel that LL parsing is easier for students to learn and thus allows them to get on to *using* the parsing technique as quickly as possible. Obviously, an instructor who favors use of LR parsing could switch the ordering. In either case, we favor waiting until the end of the course to cover the parsing method not used in the project, so that the course material germane to the project can be covered as early in the term as possible. Similarly, in the first outline below, the symbol table chapter is covered right after parsing in order to support the necessary sequencing of project work in a 10 week term.

The allocation of topics by weeks in these outlines is, of course, approximate. The entries in the "Readings" column refer either to whole chapters or sections from *Crafting a Compiler* that can be covered in roughly the time allocated. Note in particular that the selected sections from Chapters 10-13 in the first and second outlines cover a set of features that add up to a language somewhat simpler than Pascal. The second project of the three described in the next section is based on implementation of some or all of this set of features.

3.1. Senior-Level 10 Week Introductory Course

Week	Topic	Readings
1	Introduction; overview of syntax-directed translation	Ch. 1 & 2
2	Lexical analysis; grammars	3.1-3.3, 3.5, 4.1-4.3
3	Recursive descent and LL(1) parsing	4.4, 4.5, 5.1-5.8
4	Symbol tables	8.1-8.4
5	Semantic processing fundamentals;	7.1, 7.2.1, 7.3
	Storage management	9.1-9.4
6	Semantic processing: variables, types, expressions,	

	and simple control structures	10.1-10.2.2, 11.1-11.2.2, 12.1-12.3
7	Semantic processing: procedures	13.1-13.4
8	Semantic processing: records and arrays	10.2.3-10.2.4, 11.2.3-11.2.5
9	Semantic processing: packages and pointers	10.3.6, 10.3.7, 11.3.4
10	LR(1) parsing	6.1-6.6
	or	
	Code generation; intro to optimization	15.1-15.4, 16.1

3.2. Senior-Level 14 Week Introductory Course

Week	Topic	Readings
1	Introduction; overview of syntax-directed translation	Ch. 1 & 2
2	Lexical analysis; grammars	3.1-3.3, 3.5, 4.1-4.3
3	Recursive descent and LL(1) parsing	4.4, 4.5, 5.1-5.8
4	Semantic processing fundamentals;	7.1, 7.2.1, 7.3
5	Symbol tables	8.1-8.4
	Storage management	9.1-9.4
6	Semantic processing: variables, types, expressions,	
	and simple control structures	10.1-10.2.2, 11.1-11.2.2, 12.1-12.3
7	Semantic processing: records and arrays	10.2.3-10.2.4, 11.2.3-11.2.5
8	Semantic processing: procedures	13.1-13.4
9	Semantic processing: packages and pointers	10.3.6, 10.3.7, 11.3.4
10	Code generation and local optimization	15.1-15.7
11	Global optimization	16 (selected material)
12	LR(1) parsing	6.1-6.6
13	Semantic processing: advanced features	10.3, 11.3, 12.4-12.7
		(selected material)
14	More semantic processing or optimization	

3.3. Graduate-Level 14 Week Course

Week	Topic	Readings
1	Introduction; overview of syntax-directed translation	Ch. 1 & 2
2	Lexical analysis; grammars	Ch. 3
3	Grammars, recursive descent and LL(1) parsing	Ch 4, 5.1-5.8
4	Table compaction and error repair	17.1, 17.2.1-17.2.7
	Semantic processing fundamentals;	Ch. 7
5	Symbol tables	Ch. 8
	Storage management	Ch. 9
6&7	Semantic processing: declarations	Ch. 10

8&9	Semantic processing: expressions and data references	Ch. 11
10	Semantic processing: control structures	Ch. 12
11	Semantic processing: procedures	Ch. 13
12	Code generation and local optimization	15.1-15.7
13	Global optimization	16 (selected material)
14	LR(1) parsing	6.1-6.6

4. Project Software

Following is a description of the software available for distribution free of charge to adopters of *Crafting a Compiler*. All of the items listed below are written in standard Pascal and are available on a 9-track tape. The simple compilers and associated tools described in item 5 are also available in a TurboPascal version distributed on IBM PC-compatible floppy disks. Contact your Addison Wesley/Benjamin Cummings sales representative for details.

In the future, we hope to offer Ada and Modula-2 versions of much of this software. Contributions of such translations, of other tools and of enhanced versions of our tools by anyone using our software would be welcomed. Contact one of the authors if you would like to make any such software available to other compiler course instructors.

(1) ScanGen, a scanner generator tool Source is in Pascal, ~2500 lines, with documentation and test files

(2) Two LL(1) parser generators, LLGen and FMQ. FMQ is a superset of LLGen that includes error-repair capabilities. Source is in Pascal, ~5000 lines, with documentation and test files

(3) Two LALR(1) parser generators, LALRGen and ECP. ECP is a superset of LALRGen that includes error-repair capabilities. Source is in Pascal, ~6000 lines, with documentation and test files

(4) Miscellaneous utilities (written in Pascal):

    (a) A double-offset array compacter.

    (b) An interpreter for a virtual machine similar to an IBM 360/370

    (c) Subprograms to evaluate integer and real expressions with full fault checking

    (d) Subprograms to pack and unpack instructions and strings

    (e) Subprograms to cast integers into reals and vice-versa

(5) Two simple compilers and associated tools that can be used in a course where the project assignment is to extend an existing compiler (rather than to write a compiler from scratch).

The exact contents of the distribution tape are as follows:

Scanner generator files (ScanGen):

scangen.p	— Pascal source for scangen (change MaxChar to 255 if EBCDIC is used!)
scangen.doc	— scangen documentation
ada.scan	— Ada token defs
adacs.scan	— Ada/CS token defs
babbage.scan	— Babbage (a blend of Pascal & Ada)
ex1.scan	— A very simple example
ex2.scan	— A slightly more involved example
testfile	— A simple testfile (for use with "Test" option)

LL(1) parser/error repair generator files (LLGen/FMQ):

llgen.p	— Pascal source for LLGen
fmq.p	— Pascal source for FMQ (LLGen with error repair facilities)
fmq.doc	— LLGen/FMQ documentation
fmq.install	— installation notes for LLGen/FMQ
llparse.p	— LL(1) parser and corrector
llmakeindex.p	— creates an index for LL correction tables (postprocessor for FMQ)
lladacs.bnf	— LL Babbage grammar
llbabage.bnf	— LL Babbage grammar
llpascal.bnf	— LL Pascal grammar
lldcl.bnf	— small toy grammar; good for initial testing
ptablein	— parsing tables used internally by LALRGen/ECP and LLGen/FMQ
etablein	— error correction tables used internally by LALRGen/ECP and LLGen/FMQ

LALR(1) parser/error repair generator files (LALRGen/ECP):

lalrgen.p	— Pascal source for LALRGen
ecp.p	— Pascal source for ECP
ecp.doc	— documentation for LALRGen/ECP (LALR(1) generator)
ecp.install	— installation notes for LALRGen/ECP
lrparse.p	— LALR(1) parser and corrector
lrpascal.bnf	— LALR(1) Pascal grammar
lrada.bnf	— LALR(1) Ada grammar
lrdcl.bnf	— small toy grammar; good for initial testing
ecp.bnf	— grammar defining input format for the generators

Miscellaneous utilities (written in Pascal):

(a)	double.p	— A double-offset array compacter.
(b)	interp.p	— An interpreter for a virtual machine similar to an IBM 360/370
(c)	util.p	— Subprograms to evaluate integer and real expressions with full fault checking;

> subprograms to pack and unpack instructions and strings;
> subprograms to cast integers into reals and vice-versa

A Pascal version of the Micro compiler in *Crafting a Compiler*, Chapter 2:

micro.p   — Pascal source for a Micro compiler

Georgia Tech compiler project software:

micro2.p   — the source code for a compiler for a language referred to as Micro-II,
                                  a slightly more powerful language than Micro in Chapter 2 of *Crafting a Compiler*.

micro2-grammar   — the grammar for Micro-II

micro2-gramlist   — the output listing of this grammar produced by the LL(1) parser generator gt-llgen

micro2-tables   — the set of parser tables corresponding to micro2-grammar.

micro2-codefile   — the code produced when the compiler is applied to program test0

gt-llgen.p   — source code for LL(1) parser generator used by the Micro-II compiler

gt-llgen.n   — nroff input file describing the gt-llgen generator; uses -mm macros

gt-llgen.asc   — gt-llgen document in ascii format

The Micro-II compiler generates assembly code for a machine called the MACC2. An assembler and interpreter for this machine are included:

macc2.p   — source code for the machine interpreter used by the Micro-II compiler

sam2.p   — source code for the assembler used by the Micro-II compiler

sam2.n   — nroff input file describing the sam2 assembler and the MACC2 instruction set;
                              uses -mm macros

sam2.asc   — sam2 document in ascii format

The Georgia Tech project consists of extending the Micro-II compiler to include features of a language called Macro, which is a subset of Ada/CS.

macro-grammar   — the grammar for Macro, a language which is a subset of Ada/CS

macro.n   — nroff input file describing the Macro language;

uses -mm macros

macro.asc	— Macro document in ascii format
test0	— a test program of the Micro-II compiler
test1 .. test30	— test programs for Macro
test-data1	— data for test0 and test2
test-data2	— data for test1
test-data3	— data for tests 23, 24, 26, 29, 30

5. Project Suggestions

Students should be advised that any of these projects, particularly the more difficult ones, are very complex and time-consuming. The instructor should set intermediate due dates so that students begin working on the project as quickly as possible and put a consistent level of effort into it (rather than saving it all for the end of the term).

5.1. A Simple Project

Extend the Micro compiler to include the following:

(1) Declarations: Students must define the new syntax and change the semantic processing of identifier references to require a previous declaration.

(2) Real literals and variables: The scanner must be extended to handle real literals. Addition of real variables requires extension of the symbol table routines to store a type attribute with each identifier. (Currently, only the identifiers are stored; there is no associated attribute information.) All of the semantic routines that generate code must be extended to consider the types of the literals and variables they receive as parameters.

(3) Multiplication and division: New tokens must be recognized by the scanner. The grammar must be extended to enforce operator precedence. Appropriate changes must be made in the semantic routines to handle code generation based on the new tokens.

(4) **if** and/or **while** statements: New keywords must be recognized by the scanner. The grammar must be extended to include the new constructs. Semantic routines to generate the proper tests and jumps must be added.

(5) Parameterless procedures: In addition to the usual parser and scanner extensions, the symbol table must be extended to handle nested scopes. Semantic routines generate code to manage control transfer at each point of call and at the beginning and end of each procedure body.

7

Optional additions include:

(1)   An interpreter for the assembly language produced by the compiler. If this alternative is not included, such an interpreter should be provided to the students by the instructor.

(2)   Substitution of a table-driven parser for the recursive descent parser in the Micro compiler. Students should be given a driver matching the chosen parser generator. They must run the generator to produce tables for the project language and integrate the driver with their compilers.

5.2. An Intermediate Project (Macro)

Extend the Micro-II compiler (on the tape/disks distributed by the publisher) to implement Macro (a subset of Ada/CS). Micro-II is much like Micro except that all variables and constants are floating point rather than integer, it includes multiplication and division as well as the addition and subtraction included in Micro, and it also includes simple **if** statements. A self-contained description of Macro is included with the Micro-II compiler. In brief, the following extensions are required. Point totals awarded for each of these extensions in a one-quarter senior-level course are included.

(1)   Extension of scanner to handle new tokens, rewriting grammar to handle new syntax, use of parser generator to produce new tables (20 points)

(2)   Declarations of integer and real variables (10 points)

(3)   Integer literals, expressions involving integers, I/O for integers (reals already exist), and output for strings (thus string constants are also required) (10 points)

(4)   The **loop** and **exit** statements and addition of the **else** and **elsif** parts to the **if** statement (20 points)

(5)   Recursive procedures with parameters. (8 points for simple procedures, 8 points for recursion, 12 points for parameters)

(6)   Record declarations and field references (8 points)

(7)   Array declarations and element references (12 points)

(8)   Package declarations and qualified name references (12 points)

The total number of points adds to 120. Either the result can be scaled appropriately or extra credit can be allowed for scoring over 100. In a one-quarter class, very few students score more than 100 points.

5.3. A Challenging Project (Ada/CS)

The project described in this section is used in a graduate-level one-semester course at the University of Wisconsin-Madison. The course (CS 701) may be taken with or without a companion lab course (CS 702). The scoring formulas at the end of this project description reflect this choice, as well as the fact that the students may work individually or in teams of two. The project compilers are completely written by the students, in contrast to the extension approach used in the two projects described above.

The list below assigns points to each of the features of the language, with a basic subset required of all students identified first. All of the other features are optional. The difficulty of a project based on this scheme can be adjusted by modifying the grade computation formulas.

Basic Subset (130 points)[1]

A. (100 points)

    (1)   Integer, Real, Boolean types (5 points)

    (2)   Basic expressions involving Integer, Real and Boolean types (+, −, *, /, **not**, **and**, **or**, **abs**, **mod**, **, <, <=, >, >=, =, /=) (30 points)

    (3)   Input/Output

        a.   Input of Integer, Real, Boolean scalars (5 points)

        b.   Output of String literals and Integer, Real and Boolean expressions (excluding formatting) (5 points)

    (4)   Block structure (including declaration of local variables and constants) (20 points)

    (5)   Assignment statement (10 points)

    (6)   **if**, **loop**, and **exit** statements (10, 5, 10 points respectively)

B. (30 points)
Procedures and scalar-valued functions of no arguments (including nesting and non-local variables).

Optional Features (336 points possible)

A. **loop** statements (15 points total)

    (1)   **in** and **in reverse** forms (10 points)

    (2)   **while** form (5 points)

B. Arrays (30 points total)

    (1)   One-dimensional, compile-time bounds, including First and Last attributes (10 points)

    (2)   Multi-dimensional, compile-time bounds, including First and Last attributes (5 points)

    (3)   Elaboration-time bounds (9 points)

    (4)   Subscript checking (3 points)

    (5)   Record base type (3 points)

C. Boolean short-circuit operators (**and then**, **or else**) (12 points)

D. Strings (23 points total)

    (1)   Basic string operations (string variables, string assigns, all string operators (&, Substr, etc.), I/O of strings) (10 points)

    (2)   Unbounded-length strings (5 points)

    (3)   Full garbage collection of unbounded-length strings (8 points)

E. Records (15 points total)

---

[1]Point counts listed below are in each case the maximum possible for a perfectly implemented feature.

(1)   Basic features (10 points)

(2)   Fields that are compile-time bounded arrays (2 points)

(3)   Fields that are elaboration-time sized (both arrays and records) (3 points)

F.   Procedures and functions (53 points total)

(1)   Scalar parameters (15 points)

(2)   Array arguments and array-valued functions (compile-time bounds) (7 points)

(3)   Array arguments and array-valued functions (elaboration-time bounds) (5 points)

(4)   Record arguments and record-valued functions (4 points)

(5)   Conformant array parameters (i.e. array declarations of the form
type array (T **range** <>) **of** T2) (8 points)

(6)   Array-valued functions (elaboration-sized bounds) (3 points)

(7)   Array-valued functions (conformant bounds) (4 points)

(8)   Forward definition of procedures and functions (3 points)

(9)   String arguments and string-valued functions (4 points)

G.   **case** statement (20 points total)

(1)   Jump code (10 points)

(2)   If-then-else code (4 points)

(3)   Search-table code (6 points)

H.   Constrained **subtype**s (including First and Last attributes) (10 points total)

(1)   Run-time range checks (7 points)

(2)   Compile-time range checks (3 points)

I.   Folding of scalar constant expressions (8 points)

J.   Initialized variables (10 points total)

(1)   Compile-time values, global (without run-time code) (3 points)

(2)   Compile-time values, local (2 points)

(3)   Elaboration-time values (2 points)

(4)   Record fields (3 points)

K.   Formatted writes (3 points)

L.   Enumerations (18 points total)

(1)   Declaration of enumeration types; variables, assignment, and comparison operations (9 points)

(2)   Input and Output of enumeration values (5 points)

(3)   Succ, Pred, Char, and Val attributes (4 points)

M.   Arithmetic type conversion (3 points)

N.   Qualified names (from blocks and subprograms) (3 points)

O.   Pragmata (2 points)

P.   Overloading (25 points total)

    (1)   Subprogram identifiers (18 points)

    (2)   Operators (7 points)

Q.   Packages (55 points total)

    (1)   Combined packages (containing both declaration and body parts); qualified access to visible part (20 points)

    (2)   Split packages (with distinct declaration and body parts) (5 points)

    (3)   Private types (10 points)

    (4)   Separate compilation of package bodies (20 points)

R.   Use statements (11 points)

S.   Exceptions (including **exception** declarations, **raise** statements, exception handlers, predefined exceptions). (20 points).

Scaling

The raw score (RS) calculated from the above criteria will be converted to a scaled score (SS) by the formulas below. The scaled score is then converted to a letter grade as follows:

```
96..100     : A+
87..95      : A
79..86      : AB
71..78      : B
63..70      : BC
below 63    : Unsatisfactory
```

Raw scores are converted to scaled scores as follows

I.   Single person, 701 only
    $RS \leq 150$: $SS = .4\,RS + 27$
    $RS \geq 150$: $SS = .2\,RS + 57$

II.   Two persons, 701 only, or one person, 701/702
    $RS \leq 200$: $SS = .4\,RS + 7$
    $RS \geq 200$: $SS = .2\,RS + 47$

III. Two persons, 701/702
    $RS \leq 240$: $SS = .333\,RS + 7$
    $RS \geq 240$: $SS = .167\,RS + 47$

These formulas are summarized in the following table, which gives the minimum point totals needed for grades of BC, B, AB, A, and A+.

	BC	B	AB	A	A+
I	90	110	130	150	195
II	140	160	180	200	245
III	168	192	216	240	293

Students may be allowed to add features of their own (for extra credit, of course). Possible extensions to the project include:

- Language extensions — input/output of arrays, external procedures, sets, procedures as arguments, extended data types.

- Program optimizations — Eliminating redundant operations, storing frequently used variables or expressions in registers, optimizing Boolean expressions, constant-folding.

- High-quality compile-time and run-time diagnostics — "Syntax error: operator expected," or "Subscript out of range in line 21; illegal value: 137." Some form of syntactic error repair might be included.

6. Selected Solutions

A comprehensive set of problem solutions appears below. In most cases, solutions are presented in considerable detail. In a few cases (usually those requiring programming), an outline of key points is given.

6.1. Chapter 3 Solutions

1. Assume the following text is presented to a Pascal scanner:

```
program m(output);
const
   pay=284.00;
var
   bal:real;
   month:0..60;
begin
   month:=0;
   bal:=11163.05;
   while bal>0 do begin
        writeln('Month: ', month:2, ' Balance: ', bal:10:2);
        bal:=bal-(pay-0.015*bal);
        month:=month+1;
   end;
end.
```

What is the token sequence that is produced? For which tokens must the token text be returned with the token code?

Ans: The token sequence produced (using symbolic token codes) is:

program	Id("m")	(	Id("output")	)
;	**const**	Id("pay")	=	Real("284.00")
;	**var**	Id("bal")	:	Id("real")
;	Id("month")	:	Integer("0")	..
Integer("60")	;	**begin**	Id("month")	:=
Integer("0")	;	Id("bal")	:=	Real("11163.05")
;	**while**	Id("bal")	>	Integer("0")
do	**begin**	Id("writeln")	(	String("Month:")
	Id("month")	:	Integer("2")	,
String("Balance:")	,	Id("bal")	:	Integer("10")
:	Integer("2")	)	;	Id("bal")
:=	Id("bal")	-	(	Id("pay")
-	Real("0.015")	*	Id("bal")	)
;	Id("month")	:=	Id("month")	+
Integer("1")	;	**end**	;	**end**
.	Eof			

For tokens that have *semantic significance*, such as tokens for Id (identifiers), Integer (integer literals), Real (real literals), and String (string literals) in this case, the token text must be returned with the token code.

2.   How many lexical errors, if any, appear in the following Pascal fragment? How should each error be handled by the scanner?

        If a = 1. Then b :=1.0else c := 1.0E+N;
        Writeln("'","Hi there!","'");

Ans: There are three lexical errors in the given Pascal fragment (assuming the identifiers and reserved words are case insignificant) as indicated below:

        If a = 1. Then b := 1.0else c := 1.0E+N;
        e --------↑(1)--------------↑(2)--------------↑(3)
         Writeln("'","Hi there!","'");

        Errors:
        (1) Digits required after decimal point
        (2) Digits required in exponent
        (3) Digits required in exponent

A uniform way to do lexical error recovery is to buffer the scanner states along with input characters. Whenever an error occurs, we just backup the characters (and states) until a final state of some token is reached, then simply return that token and rescan from the character immediately after the token. If no final state is found in the above process, we delete the first character and rescan.

For efficiency and perhaps other more important purposes (e.g. to give more meaningful error repair for certain special cases), *ad hoc* error handling techniques are generally used (such as inserting zeros for possibly missing digits, adding a quote to close a possibly runaway string), the above uniform method could then be used as a solid last resort.

For the Pascal fragment given above, we can see that the blind backup-and-rescan approach does not give satisfactory repairs for errors (1) and (3) because they will immediately trigger syntax errors (a "dot" in illegal context, and an identifier E follows a real literal). Ideally, we would like to insert a digit at (1), to replace N by a digit at (3), and to back up scanning before else at (2). However, in practice a real scanner might just uniformly repair all above errors by inserting zero digits.

3.   Write regular expressions that define the strings recognized by the following finite automata:

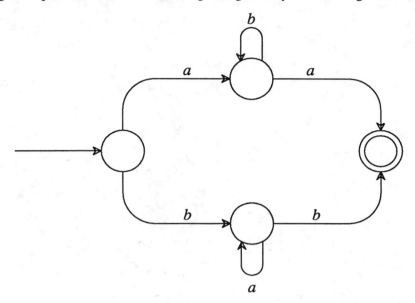

Ans: ab*a | ba*b

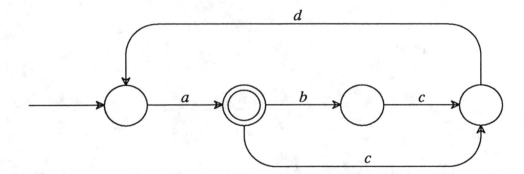

Ans: a(bcda | cda)*

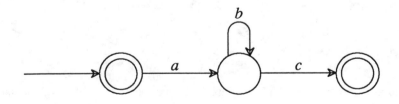

Ans: λ | ab*c

4. Write deterministic finite automata that recognize the tokens defined by the following regular expressions:

    (a) (a | (bc)*d)+

Ans:

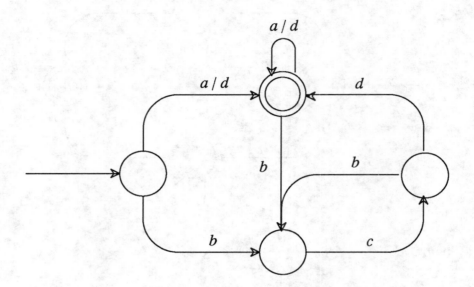

    (c) (a Not(a))*aaa

Ans:

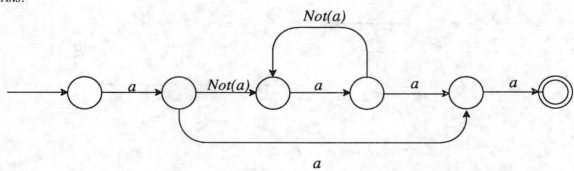

5. Write a regular expression that defines a Pascal-like fixed-decimal literal with no superfluous leading or trailing zeroes. That is, 0.0, 123.01, and 123005.0 are legal, but 00.0, 001.000, and 002345.1000 are illegal.

Ans: (in Lex notation)

    ([0-9] | [1-9][0-9]+) "." ([0-9] | [0-9]+[1-9])

6.   Write a regular expression that defines a Pascal-like comment delimited by (* and *). Individual *'s and)'s may appear in the comment body, but the pair *) may not.

Ans: (in Lex notation)

        "(*" ([^*] | [*]+ [^*)])* [*]+ "*)"

9.   Define a token class AlmostReserved to be those identifiers that are not reserved words, but would be if a single character were changed. Why is it useful to know that an identifier is "almost" a reserved word? How would you generalize a scanner to recognize AlmostReserved tokens as well as ordinary reserved words and identifiers?

Ans: The token class AlmostReserved is useful for repairing parsing errors that are caused possibly by misspelled reserved words. For example, when a compiler detects a syntax error, it checks if current token is in AlmostReserved, if so, and (one of) the corresponding reserved word(s) can be accepted at current parse state, then it can try to repair the error by changing current token to the reserved word. The syntactic error repair algorithm may look more "intelligent" in this way.

To recognize AlmostReserved, we add to our scanner a table AlmostReservedTable, in addition to the usual reserved-words table, where the entries are "patterns" for *partially* matched reserved words. For example, if we only want to match reserved words with a single character changed (i.e. replaced by some other character), such as began instead of begin, then for each reserved word $R = R_1R_2 \cdots R_n$ (R_i's are individual characters of R) we add entries $?R_2R_3 \cdots R_n$, $R_1?R_3 \cdots R_n$, ..., $R_1R_2 \cdots R_{n-1}?$, where "?" is not a legal character in either reserved words or identifiers, to the table. Now every time the scanner sees an identifier $N = N_1N_2 \cdots N_m$, first it uses the exact text to check if N is a reserved word, if not, then it checks if N is in AlmostReserved by looking up, in turn, $?N_2 \cdots N_m$, $N_1? \cdots N_m$, ..., $N_1 \cdots N_{m-1}?$ in the AlmostReservedTable (note that "?" must match a "?" in the lookup); if it's found there then N is AlmostReserved, otherwise it is an ordinary identifier.

Naturally, we assume that an entry of AlmostReservedTable, once found, lists the reserved word(s) it can match with. (For example, in Pascal, the entry for "?o" may list do and to).

10.   When a compiler is first designed and implemented, it is wise to concentrate on correctness and simplicity of design. After the compiler is fully implemented and tested, it may be necessary to increase compilation speed.

How would you determine whether the scanner component of a compiler is a significant performance bottleneck? If it is, what might you do to improve performance (without affecting compiler correctness)?

Ans: By comparing the relative speed of a compiler with syntactic and semantic processing turned on and off, we should be able to get a fairly good idea about whether the scanner component is a significant performance bottleneck. To be more accurate, we could use some kind of "profiling" tools to find out exactly which procedures that made up the bottleneck.

Once it is determined that the scanner is the bottleneck, there are a number of possible ways to improve its performance. Some of them are:

(1) Use a faster algorithm for looking up reserved words. For example, we could use perfect (one probe) hashing instead of linear or binary search.

(2) Use a more efficient data structure for storing transition table. For example, use one dimensional array instead of two dimensional one, use uncompacted table instead of a compacted one.

(3) Other (less attractive) approaches include coding critical parts of the scanner in assembly language, and using fixed-size, static, allocation for line buffers.

11.   Normally compilers can produce a source listing of the program being compiled. This listing is usually a just a copy of the source file, perhaps embellished with line numbers and page breaks.

Assume we wish to produce a pretty-printed listing (that is, a listing with text properly indented, **begin**-**end** pairs aligned, etc). How would you modify a ScanGen driver to produce a pretty-printed listing? What would you do in Lex, where a complete scanner module is produced by the Lex processor?

How are compiler diagnostics and line numbering complicated when a pretty-printed listing is produced?

Ans: We could change the ScanGen driver to, after recognizing a token, either call some pretty-printing action routine directly or call the pretty-printing driver with certain pretty-printing command. Where the pretty-printing routines or commands can be stored in a table and indexed by the kind of tokens. So, instead of echoing the input directly, ScanGen driver will simply call the proper pretty-printing routine with proper arguments for each token.

In the case of Lex, we may put the code or calls to the code for actual pretty-printing into the actions for each of the regular expressions. Or, we can wrap the generated scanner by another function which will call the scanner to get a token and do proper pretty-printing action according to the token got before returning to its caller.

When a pretty-printed listing is produced, compiler diagnostics and line numbering become more complicated because one source line may be pretty-printed as multi-lines and a single pretty-printed line may represent more than one source line. To make the listings more helpful to the users, the pretty-printer may have to produce original source line numbers along with the pretty-printed listing for easier cross reference. Also, the pretty-printer may have to associate the actual printing position with each token so that compiler diagnostics can be given with reference to the correct positions in the listing.

12.   For most modern programming languages, scanners require little context information. That is, a token can be recognized by examining its text and perhaps one or two lookahead characters. As discussed in Section 3.5, in Ada additional context is required to distinguish between a single tic, comprising an attribute symbol, and a tic, character, tic sequence, comprising a quoted character.

Assume that a flag CanParseChar is set by the parser when a quoted character can be parsed. If the next input character is a tic, CanParseChar can be used to control how the tic is scanned.

Explain how the CanParseChar flag can be *cleanly* integrated into a ScanGen- or Lex-created scanner. The changes you suggest should not unnecessarily complicate or slow the scanning of ordinary tokens.

Ans: For a ScanGen created scanner, there are two equally attractive approaches:

(1)   We can define a *pseudocharacter,* say "CharQuote", in our character class definition. And in the token definition for character literal, we use CharQuote instead of tic as the open and close quote character. In the routine CurrentChar for reading input, we add code to check if current input character is a "tic", if so and CanParseChar is set then we return "CharQuote" instead of the tic.

(2)   We can make "tic" an illegal character in our definition, and let the lexical error handling routine check if the error character is a tic, if so and CanParseChar is set, it returns the next character as a character literal token, otherwise it returns the tic or handles the (real) error.

For Lex created scanners, we just put the special checking and handling code needed for the tic character into the scanner definitions as part of the action routine to be called upon recognizing a tic.

13.   Unlike Pascal and Ada, Fortran generally ignores blanks, and may hence need extensive lookahead to determine how to scan an input line. We noted earlier a famous example of this: DO 10 I = 1 , 10 produces 7 tokens, whereas DO 10 I = 1 . 10 produces 3 tokens. How would you design a scanner to handle the extended lookahead that Fortran requires?

Ans: For each blank space, a Fortran scanner can either use it as a token separator (in addition to the normal token delimiters such as commas and parentheses) or can choose to ignore it. For example, DO I can be read as two tokens, DO and I, or a single token DOI. Therefore, for each statement (remember Fortran is a statement-oriented language and there is a limit on the maximum length of a statement), there are a set of different token sequences according to how each blank space in the statement is treated. We could then design a scanner to always return a list of possible token sequences for each statement. To be more effective, the list can be constructed incrementally by the scanner as demanded. Now the parser simply calls the scanner to generate the token sequences for a statement one by one until it can find a correct parse for that statement.

Another approach would be first to throw away all blanks in a statement, then use regular expressions with extended right context to scan for each kind of tokens. For example, we may use the following expression to recognize (somewhat simplified) DO statements:

DO ({letter} | {digit})* = ({letter} | {digit})* ","

Actually, Lex allows one to specify tokens with constraints on their right context by a special notation r1/r2 which will match a token of regular expression r1 only if its right context matches regular expression r2. The regular expression definition in Lex for matching the keyword DO would be

DO/(({letter} | {digit})* = ({letter} | {digit})* ",")

In any case, an input buffer large enough to hold the maximum length of a statement is needed to handle the extended lookahead.

14. Because Fortran generally ignores blanks, a character sequence containing n blanks can be scanned as many as 2^n different ways. Are each of these alternatives equally probable? If not, how would you alter the design you proposed in Exercise 13 to examine the most probable alternatives first?

Ans: Since most programmers tend to use blank spaces judiciously as a way to visually separate tokens, it seems that treating blanks as token separators is the most plausible first choice by a scanner. We can make the scanner we proposed in exercise 13 always return the token sequences in the order of increasing number of blank spaces ignored. That is, first we try to use all blanks as separators, then we ignore one blank space, then two blanks and so on. In this way a correct parse is very likely to be found more efficiently than a randomly generated token sequences.

15. Assume we are designing the ultimate programming language, "Utopia 86." We have already specified the language's tokens, using regular expressions, and the language's syntax, using a context-free grammar.

Now we wish to determine those token sequences that require white space to separate them (like **begin** A) and those that require extra lookahead while scanning (like 1..10). Explain how we could use the regular expressions and context-free grammar to *automatically* find all token pairs that need special handling.

Ans: First, by using algorithms similar to the ones described in Section 4.5 (Grammar Analysis Algorithms), we could compute the Follow set for each *token* (instead of for each nonterminal as in Section 4.5) from the context-free grammar definition of "Utopia 86." Where Follow(t) is defined as the set of tokens that can possibly follow token t in the language. Also using similar techniques, but from the regular expressions of "Utopia 86," we could compute the sets First1 and First2 for each token, where First1(t) is the set of possible first *character* for token t and First2(t) is the set of possible first *two* characters for token t.

Now for each token s with follow set $\{t_1,...,t_s\}$, we concatenate the regular expressions for s and each member in First1 and First2 of t_j, and try to match the new regular expressions with (the regular expression of) each token r (including s) defined in "Utopia 86."

There are two special cases to be considered for our purpose:

(1)   If s First1(t) could possibly be a "prefix" (see below) of some r, then we need white space to separate s from t in general. However, a subset of this case could be resolved not by mandatory white space but by extra lookahead character. This is the case below.

(2)   If none of s First2(t) is possibly a prefix of any r, we can use one more lookahead character to separate s from t if no white space is used to separate them.

How then are we going to check for possible prefix condition between two regular expressions s and t ? This can be done by using the idea of "cross product" finite automata. Let S(T) be a deterministic finite automaton for the regular expression s(t), and ST be the cross product automaton to be constructed (from S and T). Each state of ST is a pair of states from S and T, a state (s_i, t_j) in ST has a transition upon symbol c to state (s_k, t_l) if and only if S has a transition from s_i to s_k upon c and T has a transition from t_j to t_l upon c. ST can be constructed by first create its start state as a pair of the two start states of S and T, then add possible transitions as described above until no more transitions (and states) can be added. Now S is "possibly" a prefix of T, if there are some (final, nonerror) states in ST and, S is not possible to be a prefix of T, if there is no (final, nonerror) state in ST.

16.   Show that the set $\{[^i]^i \mid i \geq 1\}$ is not regular. Hint: Show that no fixed number of finite automaton states is sufficient to exactly match left and right brackets.

Ans: (Outline) Suppose the set $\{[^i]^i \mid i \geq 1\}$ is regular, and it is recognized by some finite state automaton F with some finite number of states say, n. Now F must accept $[^{n+1}]^{n+1}$, where n is the number of states of F, because it is of pattern $[^i]^i, i \geq 1$.

Since each state transition of F matches only one symbol, for F to accept $[^{n+1}]^{n+1}$, there must be some cycle of [-transitions in F in order to match $[^{n+1}$ alone. But if there is a cycle of length k (k > 0) of [-transitions in F when recognizing $[^{n+1}]^{n+1}$, F must also recognize $[^j ([^k)^* [^l]^{n+1}$, where $j, l \geq 0$ and $j + m{\times}k + l = n+1$ for some m > 1. Clearly, there are many strings of the above form but not of the form $[^i]^i$, which means F does not exactly recognize the set $\{[^i]^i \mid i \geq 1\}$. This contradicts our assumption and no such F exists. Since no finite automaton can be constructed to accept the set, it is not regular.

For a more formal proof, consult any text book on formal languages and automata theory. (It is usually proved using a theorem called *pumping lemma*.)

18.   Consider the following regular expression:

$$(0 \mid 1)^* 0 (0 \mid 1) (0 \mid 1) (0 \mid 1) \cdots (0 \mid 1)$$

Display the nondeterministic finite automaton corresponding to this expression.

Ans: Here is a simplified (λ-transition free) nondeterministic finite automaton for the above regular expression (there are two possible transitions for "0" from the start state):

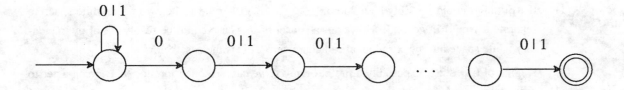

Show that the equivalent deterministic finite automaton is exponentially bigger than the nondeterministic finite automaton you presented.

Ans: (Outline) Suppose there are n stages of (0 | 1) following the single 0 in the above regular expression, we claim that the corresponding deterministic finite automaton needs at least 2^{n+1} states.

To see why this is the case, we can look at the pattern of the strings to be accepted by the automaton: they must be a string of 0 or 1 of at least $n+1$ symbols and its $n+1$st symbol from the *last* one must be a 0. Now in order to keep track of the $n+1$st symbol from the last one as the automaton is reading the input, it must also keep track of the last n symbols of the input. Because any one of the last n symbols could potentially become *the* $n+1$st symbol from the last one as long as there are more input symbols. We need one state to represent each possible configuration of the last $n+1$ symbols at any moment. Since each symbol could be either 0 or 1, there are 2^{n+1} distinct configurations in total, thus 2^{n+1} states are needed.

Note that among those 2^{n+1} states, half of them are final states. Also, the automaton needs more states to keep track of input strings which have less than $n+1$ symbols.

As we can easily see from the figure for the nondeterministic finite automaton, it only needs states of order n. We conclude that the equivalent deterministic finite automaton is exponentially bigger than the nondeterministic one.

19. Translation of a regular expression into an NFA is fast and simple. Creation of an equivalent DFA is slower, and can lead to a much larger automaton.

An interesting alternative is to scan using NFA's, obviating the need to ever build a DFA. The idea is to mimic the operation of the Close and MakeDeterministic routines (as defined in Section 3.6.1) while scanning. Rather than maintaining a single "current state," a set of possible states is maintained. As characters are read, transitions from each state in the current set are followed, creating a new set of states. If any state in the current set is final, the characters read comprise a valid token.

Define a suitable encoding for an NFA (perhaps a generalization of the transition table used for DFA's) and write a scanner driver that can use this encoding, following the "set of states" approach outlined above.

This approach to scanning will surely be slower than the standard approach that uses DFA's. Under what circumstances is scanning using NFA's attractive?

Ans: First we observe that any NFA N constructed from some regular expression R using the method described in Section 3.6 has the following important properties:

(1)   N has exactly one initial state and one final state. The final state has no outgoing transitions.

(2)   Each state of N has either one outgoing transition on a symbol in V or at most two outgoing λ-transitions.

Making use of the above properties, we could represent the transition table of an NFA with n states by just $2 \times n$ entries instead of $n \times |V|$ entries. For each state we either store the symbol it can read and the next state after seeing that symbol, or we store *at most* two next states for λ-transitions. This could be done easily with proper encoding scheme, for example, using positive integers for symbols, negative integers for states, and zero for empty entry (in case there is only one λ-transition). In the case of only single λ-transition, we could also fill in the two entries with the same next (λ-transition) state, then there is no need to check for the special case of empty entries.

The following scanner driver essentially mimics the operations of Close and MakeDeterministic on the fly. It uses a temporary stack for computing λ-closures and two "set" variables (which can be represented as bit vectors or boolean arrays) for holding current and next set of NFA states.

```
— Scan input using NFA's
procedure NFA_Scan(N : in NFA_Transition_Table; accepted: out Boolean) is
    S, T : set of NFA_State;
    c : Char;

    — Local procedure for computing λ-closure
    procedure Close(S : in out set of NFA_States) is
        R : stack of NFA_State;     — states to be examined
        s, t1, t2 : NFA_State;
    begin
        Push all states of S onto R;
        while R is not empty loop
                s := Pop(R);
                if N.state(s) has a λ-transition to t1 and t1 ∉ S then
                        Push(t1);
                        S := S ∪ { t1 };
                end if;
                if N.state(s) has another λ-transition to t2 and t2 ∉ S then
                        Push(t2);
                        S := S ∪ { t2 };
                end if;
            end loop;
        end Close;

    begin  — NFA_Scan
        S := { N.initial_state };
        Close(S);
        c := read_char();        — get next input character
        while c /= End_Of_Input loop
            T := {};
            for each state x ∈ S loop
                if N.state(x) transits to state y upon c then
                        T := T ∪ { y };
                end if;
            end loop;
            Close(T);
            S := T;
            c = read_char();
        end loop
        — at the end of input, check if it's accepted
        if N.final_state ∈ S then
                accepted := True;
        else
                accepted := False;
        end if;
    end NFA_Scan;
```

This approach of scanning using NFA's could be very attractive under circumstances that usually require only one-shot use of a regular expression for searching patterns in generally not very long input strings. Examples are text editors, and simple string pattern searching utilities.

20.   Assume R is any regular expression. **Not**(R) represents the set of all strings not in the regular set defined by R. Show that **Not**(R) is a regular set.

Hint: If R is a regular expression, there is finite automaton that recognizes the set defined by R. Transform this finite automaton into one that will recognize **Not**(R).

Ans: Let FA be an automaton that recognizes the set defined by R. Assume FA already has an explicit error state (if not, we can easily add one to it). We can now transform it into another automaton FA′ by:

(1) interchanging (renaming) the final and non-final states

(2) making the error state to be also a final state

Now FA′ recognizes **Not**(R) because whenever an input string that is accepted by FA (i.e. it stops at some final state of FA) will stop at the corresponding non-final state of FA′ and be rejected, and whenever an input string that is rejected by FA (i.e. it stops at either the error state or some non-final state of FA) will stop at the corresponding final state of FA′ and be accepted. Hence **Not**(R) is a regular set.

21. Let Rev be the operator that reverses strings. For example, Rev(abc) = cba. Let R be any regular expression. Rev(R) is the set of strings denoted by R, with each string reversed. Is Rev(R) a regular set? Why?

Ans: Yes, Rev(R) is a regular set.

(Outline) Given a regular expression R that denotes a regular set X, we could construct a regular expression R^r that denotes the set Rev(R), i.e. the set X with each string reversed, as follows:

(a) If $R = \phi$ or λ or s, where $s \in V$ (i.e., a string of length one), then $R^r = R$.

(b) If $R = S^*$, then $R^r = (S^r)^*$.

(c) If $R = S \mid T$, then $R^r = S^r \mid T^r$.

(d) If $R = ST$, then $R^r = T^r S^r$. (Note the change of order)

This can be proved by (structural) induction on the form of R and the definition of Rev. Since Rev(R) is denoted by the regular expression R^r, it is a regular set.

22. Prove that the DFA constructed by MakeDeterministic in Section 3.6.1 is equivalent to the original NFA. To do so you must show that an input string can lead to a final state in the NFA if and only if that same string will lead to a final state in the corresponding DFA.

Ans: (Outline) First we establish a lemma which says that: After reading input $c_1 c_2 \cdots c_n$ an NFA N could possibly reach any of the set of states $\{s_1, s_2, ..., s_i\}$ if and only if the same input will lead to a state S, in a corresponding DFA M, which "encodes" (in the sense of the *subset construction* algorithm presented in Section 3.6.1) that set of states of N. This can be proved by induction on the length of input and the definition of MakeDeterministic and Close in Section 3.6.1.

Using the above lemma and the definition of final states of DFA M with respect to the final state of NFA N given in MakeDeterministic, we easily conclude that an input string can lead to a final state in the NFA if and only if that same string will lead to a final state in the corresponding DFA.

6.2. Chapter 4 Solutions

2.   Take the CFG that defines Micro (in either extended or standard form) and extend it to include an equality operator, '=', and an exponentiation operator, '**'. Equal should have a lower operator precedence than plus and minus, while exponentiation should have a higher precedence. That is, A+B**2=C+D should be equivalent to (A+(B**2))=(C+D). Further, exponentiation should group from the right (so that A**B**C is equivalent to A**(B**C)), and equal should not group at all (A=B=C is illegal). Be sure that your grammar is unambiguous.

Ans: Change productions 8 to this:

    <arithexpr> —> <term> { <addop> <term> }

Add these productions to the grammar:

    <expr>   —> <arithexpr>
         —> <boolexpr>
    <boolexpr> —> <arithexpr> = <arithexpr>
    <term>   —> <primary> { ** <primary> }

4.   A production of the form $A \longrightarrow A\alpha$ is said to be *left-recursive*. Similarly, a production of the form $B \longrightarrow \beta B$ is said to be *right-recursive*.

Show that any grammar that contains both left- and right-recursive productions with the same left-hand side symbol must be ambiguous.

Ans: By assumption the grammar has productions of the form $A \longrightarrow A\alpha$ and $A \longrightarrow \beta A$. In this grammar, $A \Longrightarrow^* \beta A\alpha$. But to derive this sentential form from A, the productions can be applied in either order, generating two distinct parse trees.

5.   Assume we wish to generate a list of options chosen from a set of n choices, $\{O_1, \ldots, O_n\}$. The list can contain any subset of options, in any order, but no option may be repeated. Write a context-free grammar that generates lists of the desired form.

What is the relation between the size of your grammar and n, the number of possible options?

Is your grammar simplified or made more complicated if we further require that the options appear in a particular order (i.e. O_i can appear before O_j only if $i<j$)?

Ans: Introduce 2^n nonterminals A_R, one for each $R \subset \{1,2,...,n\}$. Include productions of the form $A_R \longrightarrow O_i A_{R \cup \{i\}}$ for each $R \in \{1,2,...,n\}$ and each $i \notin R$. Also include $A_R \longrightarrow \lambda$ for each R. Within a constant factor, there are $n(2^n)$ productions. If you require the options to be listed in order you can get away with about n^2 productions. Introduce $n+1$ nonterminals B_i, one for each $i \in \{1,2,...,n+1\}$. Include productions of the form $B_i \longrightarrow O_j B_{j+1}$ for each $j \in \{i,...,n\}$.

7.   A CFG is reduced by removing useless non-terminals and productions involving useless non-terminals. We may reduce a grammar by first removing non-terminals not reachable from the start symbol, and next removing non-terminals that do not derive any terminal string. Alternatively, we might first remove non-terminals that derive no terminal string, and then remove unreachable non-terminals.

Are these two alternatives equivalent? If not, which order is preferable?

Ans: These two approaches are not equivalent. Removing non-terminals that derive no terminal string can change other non-terminals from being reachable from the start symbol to being unreachable from the start symbol. Consider the following example grammar.

```
S  → A
S  → B
B  → B C
C  → c
A  → a
```

If we first remove non-terminals that are unreachable from the start symbol, S, no non-terminals are removed. Subsequently removing non-terminals that derive no terminal strings, we are left with the following grammar.

```
S  → A
C  → c
A  → a
```

This is not fully reduced, since C is not reachable from S. On the other hand, by first removing the non-terminals that derive no terminal strings, we then can remove all the unreachable non-terminals to yield this fully reduced grammar.

```
S  → A
A  → a
```

Happily, no similar problem arises with doing the reduction steps in this order. Removing unreachable non-terminals cannot make remaining non-terminals change from deriving a terminal string to not deriving a terminal string.

8.   Outline a proof that FillFirstSet correctly computes FirstSet values for all vocabulary symbols.

Ans: There are two parts. We must show that the symbols placed in FirstSet should be, and that the symbols that should be placed in FirstSet are.

To show that the symbols placed in FirstSet should be, use induction on the number of the iteration in the last loop of FillFirstSet at which the symbol is added. Appeal to the induction hypothesis to show that all the right-hand side symbols that claim to derive lambda actually do and to get a derivation from the RHS symbols that provide the contribution of this iteration to the FirstSet. Using those derivations it is straight forward to construct a witness derivation for the newly added symbols.

To show the converse, use induction on the depth of the derivation.

9.   Let G be any CFG and assume that $\lambda \notin L(G)$. Show that G can be transformed into an equivalent CFG that uses no λ-productions.

Ans: Determine which non-terminals can derive λ. For each non-terminal, B, that can derive λ, duplicate all the productions using B in their RHS, except omit the occurrence of B in the new copy. If a new production still contains non-terminals that can derive λ, repeat the above process. (If the righthand side of a production contains n non-terminals that can derive λ, 2^n-1 new productions will be added.) Finally, delete all λ-productions. (The grammar may now need to be reduced.) Termination and correctness are obvious.

10.   A *unit production* is a production of the form $A \rightarrow B$ where B is a single non-terminal. Show that any CFG containing unit productions can be transformed into an equivalent CFG that uses no unit productions.

Ans: To remove unit productions notice that they define a binary relation on non-terminals. Add more unit productions to the grammar to form the transitive closure of the relation defined by the original unit productions. Now, considering each unit production (of the form $A \rightarrow B$) in turn, duplicate all non-unit productions in which A appears on the RHS, substituting B for A in the new copy. The unit productions can now be removed. (The new grammar may need to be reduced.)

Termination is not difficult to show when we approach the problem this way. If we did not form the transitive closure, we would have to repeat the process on new unit-productions, and ensuring termination would become an issue.

It is straightforward to find corresponding derivations between the new and the old grammars. So the new grammar is equivalent.

11.   Some CFGs generate languages that have an infinite size, while others generate a language of finite size. Write an algorithm that tests whether a given CFG generates an infinite language.

Hint — Use the results of exercises 9 and 10 to simplify the analysis.

Ans: The method of exercise 9 can be extended to handle grammars G for which $\lambda \in L(G)$ by simply adding a new start symbol, S, and the productions $S \rightarrow \lambda$ and $S \rightarrow OldS$, where OldS is the old start symbol. Now S is the only non-terminal that may derive λ and S does not occur in the RHS of any production. The consequence of this is that any sentential form besides S only derives sentences that are at least as long.

Suppose we are given a grammar G and we want to know whether L(G) is infinite. Assume that G′

is equivalent to G, is reduced, has no unit productions, and either there are no λ productions or there is only one: S→λ. Now if there is any recursion among the productions of G′, then L(G) is infinite, otherwise not.

If there is no recursion, derivation trees are of bounded height, so there are only finitely many sentences in the language.

If there is recursion, say on A, then any sentential form in which A occurs derives a longer sentential form in which A also occurs. That is because all RHSs in which some non-terminal occurs have length greater than one symbol. So there is an infinite increasing sequence of sentential forms. Since there are no useless symbols in a reduced grammar and we have eliminated λ productions, each sentential form derives a sentence that is at least as long as the sentential form. Since no sentence is longer than all the sentential forms in the sequence, there must be infinitely many sentences derivable from the members of that sequence.

12. Let G be an unambiguous context-free grammar without λ-productions. If x ∈ L(G), show that the number of steps needed to derive x is linear in the length of x.

Does this linearity result hold for all ambiguous context-free grammars?

Ans: The number of steps in a derivation is equal to the number of interior nodes in the derivation tree. In a tree where all interior nodes have two children there is one more leaf than there are interior nodes. Where the branching factor is higher, the number of interior nodes diminishes relative to the number of leaves. Ruling out λ-productions ensures that each leaf corresponds to a terminal, instead of to λ. The only place where the derivation tree may misbehave is where the branching factor is less than two. The problem does not rule out unit productions. But it does rule out ambiguity. So there cannot be any cycles in the unit productions. That means that there is a bound on the length of any sub-branch composed entirely of unit productions. That bound keeps the number of interior nodes linear in the number of leaves, since at least a constant fraction of the interior nodes must have branching factor of at least two.

Without excluding ambiguity the result does not hold for all derivations, since then there can be cycles of unit productions, so there exist derivations of arbitrary size for some sentences. However, the exercise says "the number of steps needed to derive x." There will still exist some derivation of linear size. In particular, if sub-branches composed entirely of unit productions do not repeat any non-terminals, then that derivation is linear. Notice that such a derivation always exists, since sub-branches with repeats can be shortened.

6.3. Chapter 5 Solutions

1.   Which of the following grammars are LL(1)? Explain why.

   (a)   S   → A B c
          A   → a
          A   → λ
          B   → b
          B   → λ

   Ans: A grammar is LL(1) if and only if the predict sets for productions that have the same left-hand side are disjoint.

Production	Predict Set
S → A B c	{a,b,c}
A → a	{a}
A → λ	{b,c}
B → b	{b}
B → λ	{c}

The grammar is LL(1).

   (b)   S   → A b
          A   → a
          A   → B
          A   → λ
          B   → b
          B   → λ

   Ans:

Production	Predict Set
S → A b	{a,b}
A → a	{a}
A → B	{b}
A → λ	{b}
B → b	{b}
B → λ	{b}

The grammar is not LL(1). The predict sets for productions 3 and 4 as well as for productions 5 and 6 are not disjoint.

(c) S → A B B A
     A → a
     A → λ
     B → b
     B → λ

Ans:

Production	Predict Set
S → A B B A	{a,b,$}
A → a	{a}
A → λ	{a,b,$}
B → b	{b}
B → λ	{a,b,$}

The grammar is not LL(1). The predict sets for productions 2 and 3 as well as for productions 4 and 5 are not disjoint.

(d) S → a S e
     S → B
     B → b B e
     B → C
     C → c C e
     C → d

Ans:

Production	Predict Set
S → a S e	{a}
S → B	{b,c,d}
B → b B e	{b}
B → C	{c,d}
C → c C e	{c}
C → d	{d}

The grammar is LL(1).

2.   Construct the LL(1) table for the following grammar:

```
1    Expr       →  – Expr
2    Expr       →  ( Expr )
3    Expr       →  Var ExprTail
4    ExprTail   →  – Expr
5    ExprTail   →  λ
6    Var        →  Id VarTail
7    VarTail    →  ( Expr )
8    VarTail    →  λ
9    Goal       →  Expr $
```

Ans:

	Id	(	)	–	$
Expr	3	2		1	
ExprTail		5	4	5	
Var	6				
VarTail		7	8	8	8
Goal	9	9		9	

3.   Trace the operation of an LL(1) parser for the grammar of exercise 2 on Id– –Id((Id)).

Ans:

Step	Parser Action	Remaining Input	Parse Stack
(1)	Predict 9	Id—Id((Id))$	Goal
(2)	Predict 3	Id—Id((Id))$	Expr $
(3)	Predict 6	Id—Id((Id))$	Var ExprTail $
(4)	Match	Id—Id((Id))$	Id VarTail ExprTail $
(5)	Predict 8	—Id((Id))$	VarTail ExprTail $
(6)	Predict 4	—Id((Id))$	ExprTail $
(7)	Match	—Id((Id))$	– Expr $
(8)	Predict 1	–Id((Id))$	Expr $
(9)	Match	–Id((Id))$	– Expr $
(10)	Predict 3	Id((Id))$	Expr $
(11)	Predict 6	Id((Id))$	Var ExprTail $
(12)	Match	Id((Id))$	Id VarTail ExprTail $
(13)	Predict 7	((Id))$	VarTail ExprTail $
(14)	Match	((Id))$	(Expr) ExprTail $
(15)	Predict 2	(Id))$	Expr) ExprTail $
(16)	Match	(Id))$	(Expr)) ExprTail $
(17)	Predict 3	Id))$	Expr)) ExprTail $
(18)	Predict 6	Id))$	Var ExprTail)) ExprTail $
(19)	Match	Id))$	Id VarTail ExprTail)) ExprTail $
(20)	Predict 8	))$	VarTail ExprTail)) ExprTail $
(21)	Predict 5	))$	ExprTail)) ExprTail $
(22)	Match	))$	)) ExprTail $
(23)	Match	)$	) ExprTail $
(24)	Predict 5	$	ExprTail $
(25)	Match	$	$

4.　　　Transform the following grammar into LL(1) form, using the techniques of Section 5.6:

1	DeclList	$\longrightarrow$ DeclList ; Decl
2	DeclList	$\longrightarrow$ Decl
3	Decl	$\longrightarrow$ IdList : Type
4	IdList	$\longrightarrow$ IdList , Id
5	IdList	$\longrightarrow$ Id
6	Type	$\longrightarrow$ ScalarType
7	Type	$\longrightarrow$ **array** (ScalarTypeList) **of** Type
8	ScalarType	$\longrightarrow$ Id
9	ScalarType	$\longrightarrow$ Bound .. Bound
10	Bound	$\longrightarrow$ Sign IntLiteral
11	Bound	$\longrightarrow$ Id
12	Sign	$\longrightarrow$ +
13	Sign	$\longrightarrow$ –
14	Sign	$\longrightarrow \lambda$
15	ScalarTypeList	$\longrightarrow$ ScalarTypeList , ScalarType
16	ScalarTypeList	$\longrightarrow$ ScalarType

Ans:　Since Id predicts production 11, it is in the predict set of both 8 and 9. To remove this prediction ambiguity, substitute the right hand sides of productions 10 and 11 for the first occurrence of Bound in production 9. Now factor out the common prefix Id according to the algorithm in Figure 5.12.

The left recursion in productions 1, 4 and 15 are removed by the transform defined in Figure 5.13. The resulting grammar is shown below:

1	DeclList	$\longrightarrow$ DeclList1 DeclList2
2	DeclList1	$\longrightarrow$ Decl
3	DeclList2	$\longrightarrow$; Decl DeclList2
4	DeclList2	$\longrightarrow \lambda$
5	Decl	$\longrightarrow$ IdList : Type
6	IdList	$\longrightarrow$ IdList1 IdList2
7	IdList1	$\longrightarrow$ Id
8	IdList2	$\longrightarrow$, Id IdList2
9	IdList2	$\longrightarrow \lambda$
10	Type	$\longrightarrow$ ScalarType
11	Type	$\longrightarrow$ **array** (ScalarTypeList) **of** Type
12	ScalarType	$\longrightarrow$ Id ScalarTypeTail
13	ScalarTypeTail	$\longrightarrow$ .. Bound
14	ScalarTypeTail	$\longrightarrow \lambda$
15	ScalarType	$\longrightarrow$ Sign IntLiteral .. Bound
16	Bound	$\longrightarrow$ Sign IntLiteral
17	Bound	$\longrightarrow$ Id
18	Sign	$\longrightarrow$ +
19	Sign	$\longrightarrow$ –
20	Sign	$\longrightarrow \lambda$
21	ScalarTypeList	$\longrightarrow$ ScalarTypeList1 ScalarTypeList2
22	ScalarTypeList1	$\longrightarrow$ ScalarType
23	ScalarTypeList2	$\longrightarrow$, ScalarType ScalarTypeList2
24	ScalarTypeList2	$\longrightarrow \lambda$

5.   Run your solution to exercise 4 through LLGen, or any other LL(1) parser generator, to verify that it actually is LL(1).

How do you know that your solution generates the same language as the original grammar?

Ans: If each individual transformation preserves the language generated by the grammar, then, by induction, any sequence of such transformations preserves the language generated by the grammar.

Consider the factoring algorithm that transforms the set of productions

$$S = \{A \longrightarrow \alpha\beta, \ldots, A \longrightarrow \alpha\zeta\}$$

with the same left-hand side, A, and a common prefix, α to the set

$$S1 = \{A \longrightarrow \alpha N, N \longrightarrow \beta, \ldots, N \longrightarrow \zeta\}$$

where N is a new non-terminal.

The language generated by any production $A \longrightarrow \alpha X, X \in \beta, \ldots, \zeta$, is generated by the productions $A \longrightarrow \alpha N$ and $N \longrightarrow X$. Hence any string in the language generated by S is included in the language generated by S1. Moreover, the set S is obtained from S1 by simply substituting for N. Hence every string in the language generated by S1 is included in the language generated by S. In other words, S and S1 generate the same language. This implies that the factoring transform preserves the language.

The left recursion removal transform replaces the set

$$S = \{A \longrightarrow A\alpha, A \longrightarrow \beta, \ldots, A \longrightarrow \zeta\}$$

with the same left-hand side, A, where A is left-recursive, with the set

$$S1 = \{A \longrightarrow N T, N \longrightarrow \beta, \ldots, N \longrightarrow \zeta, T \longrightarrow \alpha T \mid \lambda\}$$

where N and T are new non-terminals

It is easy to see that the language generated by either of the sets consists of only those strings in which any of $\beta, \ldots, \zeta$ is followed by zero or more α's. Hence each such replacement preserves the language generated.

6.   Show that every regular set can be defined by an LL(1) grammar.

Ans: Corresponding to every regular set there is a deterministic finite automaton that recognizes the strings belonging to the regular set. The steps given below construct a grammar that generates the language recognized by a deterministic finite automaton.

(1)   The input characters to the automaton are the terminals in the grammar.

(2)   For every state i in the automaton, S_i is a non-terminal in the grammar. If k is the start state of the automaton, then S_k is the start symbol of the grammar.

(3)   For every transition from state i to state j labeled with input character α, introduce a production $S_i \longrightarrow \alpha S_j$.

(4)   For every final state k, introduce the production $S_k \rightarrow \lambda$.

The deterministic character of the automaton ensures that the above grammar is LL(1). The predict sets of the λ productions contain only the end of input marker. Since the outgoing arcs from any state are uniquely labeled, the predict sets of the production with the same left hand side are disjoint. An LL(1) parser for the grammar generated as above accepts exactly the same strings that are recognized by the automaton. Every transition from state i to state j on input α corresponds to the parser steps predict $S_i \rightarrow \alpha S_j$ followed by match α. At any point, if the automaton is in state i, then the parse stack consists of the non-terminal S_i. At the end of the input, if the automaton is in a final state, the parser predicts the λ production for the non-terminal and halts.

7.   A grammar is said to have *cycles* if it is the case that $A \Rightarrow^+ A$. Show that no grammar that has cycles can be LL(1).

Ans: Let α be any string that can be derived from A. If the grammar has a cycle then α has at least two distinct derivation sequences as shown below:

$$A \Rightarrow^+ \alpha \text{ and } A \Rightarrow^+ A \Rightarrow^+ \alpha$$

Hence the grammar is ambiguous. From Section 5.9, such a grammar cannot be LL(1).

8.   In Section 5.9 it is established that LL(1) parsers operate in linear time. That is, when parsing an input, the parser requires *on average* only a constant-bounded amount of time per input symbol.

Is it ever the case that an LL(1) parser requires more than a constant-bounded amount of time to accept some particular symbol? Phrased differently, can we bound by a constant the time interval between successive calls to the scanner to get the next input token?

Ans: No. The time interval between successive calls to the scanner to get a particular input token may depend on the the length of the input string. Consider the following LL(1) grammar:

```
A   → Bb
B   → aBC
B   → λ
C   → λ
```

A parser for this grammar accepts strings with zero or more a's followed by a b. Note that for each a accepted, the non-terminal C is placed once on the parse stack. When a b is encountered, each of the Cs must be reduced to λ before the token b is matched. Since the number of Cs depends on the number of as in the input string, the time taken by the parser to accept b cannot be bounded by a constant.

9.   A grammar is in *Greibach Normal Form (GNF)* if all productions are of the form $A \rightarrow a\ \alpha$, where a is a terminal, and α is an arbitrary string of symbols. Let G be any grammar that does not generate

λ. Give an algorithm to transform G into GNF.

Ans: Let $V_n = \{A_1, A_2, ..., A_m\}$ be the set of non-terminals in the grammar.

(1) Eliminate all λ productions:

For each λ production, $A_i \longrightarrow \lambda$ and each production with A_i occurring on the right-hand side, add a production to the grammar with A_i removed from the right-hand side.

(2) Modify the productions so that if $A_i \longrightarrow A_j\alpha$, then $j > i$, for $1 \le i < m$:

Start with A_1 and proceed to A_m. Suppose the productions have been modified so that the above condition is satisfied for $1 \le i \le k$. For each production $A_{k+1} \longrightarrow A_j\, \alpha$, with $j < k+1$, generate a new set of productions by substituting for A_j the right-hand side of each production of A_j. Repeat this process for the productions of A_{k+1} until for each production of the form $A_{k+1} \longrightarrow A_l\beta$, $l \ge k+1$. If there are productions with $l = k+1$, then use the left-recursion removal transform (Figure 5.13).

(3) Convert all productions of the form $A_i \longrightarrow A_j\beta$ into the normal form:

Start with A_m and proceed to A_1. All the productions for A_m must start with a terminal. The productions of A_{m-1} start either with a terminal or A_m. For each production of A_{m-1} that starts with A_m, generate new productions by substituting the right-hand side of all productions of A_m. Now all productions of A_{m-1} start with a terminal. Repeat this process for A_{m-2} through A_1.

(4) Each non-terminal introduced by the left-recursion transform in step 2 must either begin with a terminal or one of the original non-terminals. For each production that begins with a non-terminal, generate new productions by substituting the right-hand side of all productions for that non-terminal.

10. If we take a grammar and put it into GNF using the algorithm developed in exercise 9, we know there will be no left recursion. The transformed grammar may still have common prefixes, and hence may not be LL(1). Assume we use **Factor** of Section 5.6 to factor common prefixes. The resulting grammar will have neither left recursion nor common prefixes, and hence will be "close" to LL(1) in form. Show that the absence of common prefixes and left recursion in an unambiguous grammar *does not* guarantee that a grammar will be LL(1).

Ans: Consider the example in Section 5.10:

$$S \longrightarrow aAa$$
$$S \longrightarrow bAba$$
$$A \longrightarrow b$$
$$A \longrightarrow \lambda$$

This grammar has neither left recursion nor common prefixes. However it is not LL(1) since b predicts both productions of A. Note that this grammar is LL(2) and not ambiguous.

11.   Use the techniques of Section 5.10 to create an LL(2) parser for the following grammar:

       (1) Stmt   —> Id ;
       (2) Stmt   —> Id (IdList) ;
       (3) Stmt   —> Id : Stmt
       (4) IdList —> Id
       (5) IdList —> Id , IdList

Ans: It can be easily verified that the grammar is Strong LL(2). The LL(2) table for the grammar is:

	Id;	Id(	Id)	Id:	Id,
Stmt	1	2		3	
Idlist			4		5

12.   Show that every LL(1) grammar is also Strong LL(1).

Hint: Show that any grammar that fails to satisfy the Strong LL(1) definition must also fail to satisfy the LL(1) definition.

Ans: Let G be a grammar that is not Strong LL(1). From Section 5.10, G must have two productions of the form

$$A \longrightarrow \beta, \ A \longrightarrow \gamma, \ \beta \neq \gamma$$

such that

$$\text{First}(\beta \ \text{Follow}(A)) \cap \text{First}(\gamma \ \text{Follow}(A)) \neq \phi$$

Let a be an element of both First(β Follow(A)) and First(γ Follow(A)). From the definition of First and Follow, a must belong to

First(β) or
Follow(A) if $\lambda \in$ First(β).

Suppose there exist w and α such that

$$S \Rightarrow^*_{lm} wA\alpha \Rightarrow_{lm} w\beta\alpha \Rightarrow^* wx$$
$$S \Rightarrow^*_{lm} wA\alpha \Rightarrow_{lm} w\gamma\alpha \Rightarrow^* wy$$

If a $\in$ First(β) then by definition of First there is a derivation corresponding to (1) above in which x is of the form au. If $\lambda \in$ First(β) and a $\in$ Follow(A) then there is a derivation as follows:

$$S \Rightarrow^*_{lm} wA\alpha \Rightarrow_{lm} w\beta\alpha \Rightarrow^* w\lambda a\alpha$$

In either case there exists an x such that First(x) = a. Similarly one can show that there exists a y such that First(y) = a. Hence this grammar satisfies the condition:

First(x) = First(y)

Since $\beta \neq \gamma$ from the initial hypothesis, G does not satisfy the LL(1) definition. Therefore all LL(1) grammars must be Strong LL(1).

13. Show that for every LL(k) grammar there is a Strong LL(k) grammar that generates the same language.

Hint: Consider the expanded grammar formed by creating non-terminals of the form [A,L].

Ans: Section 5.10 describes the method to obtain an equivalent grammar using non-terminals of the form [A,L].

Let G be a LL(k) grammar and G1, the grammar obtained by using the method in Section 5.10. Let $[A,L] \longrightarrow \beta$ and $[A,L] \longrightarrow \gamma$ be any two productions in G1 with the same left-hand side (if there are none, then the grammar is trivially Strong LL(k)). By using substitution and factoring transformations, one can ensure that productions in G1 with the same left-hand side do not have a common prefix of length $\geq k$. The construction of L guarantees that $L = Follow_k([A,L])$. Suppose there is a string α such that $\alpha \in (First_k(\beta x) \cap First_k(\gamma x))$ for some $x \in L$. Then at every occurrence of A in the right-hand side of a production of G corresponding to the occurrence of [A,L] in G2, α predicts both $A \longrightarrow \beta$ and $A \longrightarrow \gamma$. This implies that G is not LL(k). Therefore, if G is LL(k), $First_k(\beta x) \cap First_k(\gamma x) = \phi$ for all $x \in L$. Hence the derived grammar G1 is Strong LL(k).

14. Using the techniques of Section 5.3, write a program that reads the tables generated by LLGen and produces the corresponding recursive descent parsing procedures.

Ans: Some guidelines:

The format of the output provided by LLGen is in Appendix C.

The right-hand sides of productions in the LLGen output are reversed. RHS(P) as used in Section 5.3 must return the right-hand side in the correct order.

Avoid generating conditional logic when the nonterminal has a single production.

It may be more efficient to generate **if** statements rather than **case** statements for nonterminals that have predictions for only one or two terminals.

6.4. Chapter 6 Solutions

5. Show that the CFSM corresponding to an LL(1) grammar has the property that each configuration set has exactly one basis item, assuming all non-terminals can derive some non-empty terminal string.

Ans: We give the outline of a proof by induction on the length of the shortest path from the initial state to each other state. Since all configuration sets are reachable from the initial set in a finite number of steps such an induction can be used.

The fact that the initial set has only one basis item will form the basis of our induction. The induction step will show that, if a given configuration set has only one basis item, then all the successor sets have only one basis item. In the proof of the step we use a case analysis of the ways there might be two basis items and derive a contradiction in each case.

First notice that the only way you could get two basis items in the successor set is to have two items in the current set that have the same symbol following the dot. Call the symbol following the dot the transition symbol. Next, note that the items of the current configuration set form a directed graph whose edges indicate "requires the addition of."

There are two cases: Case One, the two items that have the same transition symbol are connected by a directed path; Case Two, they are not. Case One leads to a (possibly indirect) left recursion, and so to a contradiction of the fact that the grammar is LL(1).

Case Two is a little trickier. Note that all nodes in the graph are reachable from the node for the lone basis item. Thus it makes sense to talk about the nearest common ancestor of two nodes that do not lie on a common path.

Let $P \rightarrow \gamma \bullet C\delta$ be the nearest common ancestor of two hypothetical items, $A \rightarrow \bullet X\alpha$ and $B \rightarrow \bullet X\beta$, that do not lie on a common path. Now consider $C \rightarrow \bullet E\omega$, the successor of $P \rightarrow \gamma \bullet C\delta$ that lies on the shortest path to $A \rightarrow \bullet X\alpha$, and $C \rightarrow \bullet F\tau$, the successor of $P \rightarrow \gamma \bullet C\delta$ that lies on the shortest path to to $B \rightarrow \bullet X\beta$. $C \rightarrow \bullet E\omega$ and $C \rightarrow \bullet F\tau$ are distinct, since $P \rightarrow \gamma \bullet C\delta$ is the nearest common ancestor. But, since all non-terminals derive some non-empty string, it follows that $First(X)$ is a subset of both $First(E)$ and $First(F)$, contradicting the fact that the grammar is LL(1).

7. Which of the following grammars are LR(1)? Which are LALR(1)? Which are SLR(1)? In each case justify your categorization.

    (a) S $\rightarrow$ Id := E ;
         E $\rightarrow$ E + P
         E $\rightarrow$ P
         P $\rightarrow$ Id
         P $\rightarrow$ (E)
         P $\rightarrow$ Id := E

Ans: This grammar is not LR(1). The following configuration set occurs in the LR(1) machine.

$$P \rightarrow id := E \bullet \quad \{+, ;,)\}$$
$$E \rightarrow E \bullet + P \quad \{+, ;,)\}$$

There is a shift-reduce conflict on lookahead "+" in the state labeled with this configuration set.

(b) S   → Id := A ;
     A   → Id := A
     A   → E
     E   → E + P
     E   → P
     P   → Id
     P   → (A)

Ans: This grammar is SLR(1).

(c) S   → Id := A ;
     A   → Id := A
     A   → E
     E   → E + P
     E   → P
     E   → P +
     P   → Id
     P   → (A)

Ans: This grammar is not LR(1). The following configuration set occurs in the LR(1) machine.

$$P \rightarrow id := E \bullet \quad \{+, ;,)\}$$
$$E \rightarrow E \bullet + P \quad \{+, ;,)\}$$

There is a shift-reduce conflict on lookahead "+" in the state labeled with this configuration set.

(d) S   → Id := A ;
     A   → Pre E
     Pre → Pre Id :=
     Pre → λ
     E   → E + P
     E   → P
     P   → Id
     P   → (A)

Ans: This grammar is SLR(1).

(e)   S $\rightarrow$ Id := A ;
      A $\rightarrow$ Pre E
      Pre $\rightarrow$ Id := Pre
      Pre $\rightarrow \lambda$
      E $\rightarrow$ E + P
      E $\rightarrow$ P
      P $\rightarrow$ Id
      P $\rightarrow$ (A)

Ans: This grammar is not LR(1). The following two configurations occur in one state in the LR(1) machine.

      Pre $\rightarrow \bullet$ {id,)}
      Pre $\rightarrow \bullet$id := Pre   {id,)}

There is a shift-reduce conflict on lookahead "id" in the state with these configurations. More than one state contains a conflict for this grammar.

(f)   S $\rightarrow$ Id := A ;
      A $\rightarrow$ Id := A
      A $\rightarrow$ E
      E $\rightarrow$ E + P
      E $\rightarrow$ P
      P $\rightarrow$ Id
      P $\rightarrow$ (A ; A)
      P $\rightarrow$ (V , V)
      P $\rightarrow$ { A , A }
      P $\rightarrow$ { V ; V }
      V $\rightarrow$ Id

Ans: This grammar is not LALR(1), but it is LR(1). The following configuration state labels in one state of the LALR(1) machine.

      P $\rightarrow$ id $\bullet$ {+, ;, ,}
      V $\rightarrow$ id $\bullet$ {;, ,}
      A $\rightarrow$ id $\bullet$:= A   {;, ,}

There is a shift-reduce conflict on lookahead ";" or "," between the first two configurations. No such conflict occurs in the LR(1) machine. The configurations are divided between two states in the LR(1) machine so that upon shifting "(", the following state is reached.

      P $\rightarrow$ id $\bullet$ {;}
      V $\rightarrow$ id $\bullet$ {,}
      A $\rightarrow$ id $\bullet$:= A   {;}

This state has no conflicts. Similarly, upon shifting "{", this state is reached.

$$
\begin{array}{lll}
P & \rightarrow \text{id} \bullet & \{,\} \\
V & \rightarrow \text{id} \bullet & \{;\} \\
A & \rightarrow \text{id} \bullet := A & \{,\}
\end{array}
$$

It also has no conflicts.

(g)
$$
\begin{array}{ll}
S & \rightarrow \text{Id} := A ; \\
A & \rightarrow \text{Id} := A \\
A & \rightarrow E \\
E & \rightarrow E + P \\
E & \rightarrow P \\
P & \rightarrow \text{Id} \\
P & \rightarrow (\text{Id} ; \text{Id}) \\
P & \rightarrow (A)
\end{array}
$$

Ans: The grammar is LALR(1), but not SLR(1). The following configurations occur in one state of the SLR(1) machine.

$$
\begin{array}{lll}
P & \rightarrow \text{id} \bullet & \{+, ;,)\} \\
P & \rightarrow (\text{id} \bullet ; \text{id}) & \{+, ;,)\}
\end{array}
$$

There is a shift-reduce conflict on lookahead ";" in the state with these configurations. In the LALR(1) machine, ";" does not appear in the lookahead of these configurations, so no conflict arises.

8.   Show that the lookahead components of LR(1) configurations are exact. That is:

(a)   If state s contains an LR(1) configuration $A \rightarrow \alpha \bullet , a$ then there exists a rightmost derivation $S \Rightarrow^*_{rm} \beta A a w \Rightarrow_{rm} \beta \alpha a w$ where state s is reached after shifting $\beta \alpha$.

(b)   If there exists a rightmost derivation $S \Rightarrow^*_{rm} \beta A a w \Rightarrow_{rm} \beta \alpha a w$ then there exists a state s, reached after shifting $\beta \alpha$, that contains the configuration $A \rightarrow \alpha \bullet , a$.

Ans: The goal of this problem is to show that the LR(1) machine has exactly the states that are needed to parse according to the grammar. As usual, we will assume the grammar in question is reduced: it has no useless non-terminals.

(a)   This proof is by induction on the length of the shortest sequence of transitions from the initial state to a given state, s. By the construction of the LR(1) machine, all states are reachable from the initial state by the sequences of state transitions corresponding to shifting some sequence of symbols (terminals and nonterminals).

We will show that for all states s and all items, $A \rightarrow \gamma \bullet \omega, a$, in s, there exists a β such that $S \Rightarrow^*_{rm} \beta A a w \Rightarrow_{rm} \beta \gamma \omega a w$, where state s is reached after shifting $\beta \gamma$. This will imply the assertion we are to prove by taking $\gamma = \alpha$ and $\omega = \lambda$. As is frequently the case with induction, it is more convenient to prove a lemma that is stronger than our intended result than it is to prove the result directly. This is because it is convenient to be able to use the stronger lemma in the induction hypothesis. A direct proof method is discussed briefly below.

Induction Basis: We must show that for each configuration $A \longrightarrow \gamma \bullet \omega, a$ in the initial state there is a β such that $S \Rightarrow^*_{rm} \beta Aaw \Rightarrow_{rm} \beta\gamma\omega aw$, where the initial state is reached after shifting $\beta\gamma$.

By construction, if $A \longrightarrow \gamma \bullet \omega, a$ is in the initial state, then γ must be λ. We only have to show that there exists a suitable β. Naturally, λ is just such a choice for β, since we can get to the initial state by performing the empty sequence of state transitions.

$S \Rightarrow^*_{rm} Aaw$ must hold for some terminal string w, otherwise either there are useless symbols in the grammar or $A \longrightarrow \gamma \bullet \omega, a$ is not in the initial state, neither of which is possible. $S \Rightarrow^*_{rm} Aaw \Rightarrow_{rm} \alpha aw$ follows trivially.

Induction Step: Suppose the state s is reachable in $k+1$ transitions from the initial state. Consider any item, $A \longrightarrow \gamma \bullet \omega, a$, in s. We must show that there exists a β such that $S \Rightarrow^*_{rm} \beta Aaw \Rightarrow_{rm} \beta\gamma\omega aw$, where s is reached after shifting $\beta\gamma$. To show this, we use the induction assumption: all states s' reachable from the initial state in k state transitions have the desired property. There are two cases.

Case One: $A \longrightarrow \gamma \bullet \omega, a$ is a basis item. By construction we know there is a predecessor state in which the same item occurred, except the dot was one symbol to the left. In other words, suppose $\gamma = \delta X$. Because $A \longrightarrow \delta X \bullet \omega, a$ is a basis item in s, there must be a state s' reachable by a sequence of state transitions of length k and containing the item $A \longrightarrow \delta \bullet X\omega, a$.

By the induction assumption, there exists a β such that $S \Rightarrow^*_{rm} \beta Aaw \Rightarrow_{rm} \beta\delta X\omega aw$, and s' is reachable by shifting $\beta\delta$. From this it is trivial that $S \Rightarrow^*_{rm} \beta Aaw \Rightarrow_{rm} \beta\gamma\omega aw$ and that s is reachable by shifting $\beta\gamma$.

Case Two: $A \longrightarrow \gamma \bullet \omega, a$ is a closure item. In this case, γ must be λ. Furthermore, by the construction, there must be another item in s, $P \longrightarrow \tau \bullet A\kappa, c$, where $a \in First(\kappa c)$. Let us assume this is a basis item, and hence handled by Case One.

(In general, we have to go back through a chain of closure items, finally coming to a basis item where Case One applies. To be completely formal, Case Two must be proven by induction on the length of the chain of items starting with the basis item and ending with $A \longrightarrow \bullet \omega, a$. However, such extreme formality is not terribly enlightening. So we just prove the basis of that induction here.)

Since $P \longrightarrow \tau \bullet A\kappa, c$ is a basis item, Case One shows that there exists β' such that $S \Rightarrow^*_{rm} \beta' Pcw' \Rightarrow_{rm} \beta' \tau A\kappa cw'$, and s is reachable after shifting $\beta' \tau$. By choosing $\beta = \beta' \tau$ not only do we reach s after shifting $\beta\gamma$, but we have $S \Rightarrow^*_{rm} \beta A\kappa cw'$. Since $a \in First(\kappa c)$, there must be a terminal string aw such that $S \Rightarrow^*_{rm} \beta Aaw \Rightarrow_{rm} \beta\gamma\omega aw$.

The result is now shown.

This result can be proven directly (without proving the stronger lemma) by using strong induction. Strong induction allows us to use as the induction hypothesis that the desired property holds for all sequences of length less than or equal to k (not just equal to k). We can then omit

Case One in the induction step, where the item is a basis item. Instead, we argue that some predecessor state s' introduces $P \rightarrow \bullet \tau A \kappa, c$ as a closure item, where the s' is reachable by shifting a sequence of length $k+1-len$ where len is the length of τ. This does not simplify matters, however, since we still have to show (probably by induction on the length of τ) that we can get from s' to s by shifting τ.

(Strong induction, like the more common "weak" induction, can be viewed as a proof by contradiction based on the well-foundedness of the natural numbers: every set of natural numbers has a least element. The step can be viewed as saying the following. Suppose the property doesn't hold everywhere. Let S be the set of natural numbers where the property does not hold. S has a least element by well-foundedness. Suppose the least element is $k+1$. The step shows that "if the property holds at values less than or equal to k, then it holds at $k+1$." The contrapositive of this lemma gives us that "if the property does not hold for $k+1$, then it does not hold for some value less than or equal to k." But that contradicts the assumption that $k+1$ is the least counter example.)

(b)   Use induction on the length of $\beta\alpha$.

16.   Write a context-free grammar for the expression structure of MicroPlus as defined in Figure 6.33. The grammar you produce must enforce the operator precedence levels and associativities shown in the figure.

Ans:

$$
\begin{array}{lll}
\text{BoolExpr} & \rightarrow & \text{Expr = Expr} \\
\text{Expr} & \rightarrow & \text{Expr + Term} \\
 & \rightarrow & \text{Expr} - \text{Term} \\
 & \rightarrow & \text{Term} \\
\text{Term} & \rightarrow & \text{Term} * \text{Factor} \\
 & \rightarrow & \text{Term / Factor} \\
 & \rightarrow & \text{Factor} \\
\text{Factor} & \rightarrow & \text{id} \\
 & \rightarrow & -\text{ Factor}
\end{array}
$$

18.   In Yacc it is impossible to give precedence and associativity definitions that place left- and right-associative operators at the same precedence level. Is this an oversight, or is there a reason why such definitions are disallowed?

Ans: If both left- and right-associative operators occurred at the same precedence level, there would be ambiguity in evaluation order. For example, multiplication is left-associative and exponentiation is right-associative. Suppose we put them at the same precedence level. Then consider an expression like 4 * 2 ** 2. The value of this expression is 16 or 64 according to which operation is has precedence. But since we have given both operations the same precedence, the value of the expression is ambiguous.

19.   Assume we have a Pascal-like language that has the following control structures:

        if \<expr\> **then** \<stmt\>
        if \<expr\> **then** \<stmt\> **else** \<stmt\>
        while \<expr\> **do** \<stmt\>

Give an unambiguous LALR(1) grammar that defines these structures and correctly handles the dangling else problem.

Ans: The dangling else problem is solved correctly if each else part is contained in the most deeply nested if statement possible.

Here is an LALR(1) grammar that solves the problem.

\<stmt\>	$\longrightarrow$ \<openstmt\>
	$\longrightarrow$ \<closedstmt\>
\<openstmt\>	$\longrightarrow$ simplestmt
	$\longrightarrow$ **if** \<expr\> **then** \<openstmt\> **else** \<openstmt\>
	$\longrightarrow$ **while** \<expr\> **do** \<openstmt\>
\<closedstmt\>	$\longrightarrow$ **if** \<expr\> **then** \<stmt\>
	$\longrightarrow$ **while** \<expr\> **do** \<closedstmt\>
	$\longrightarrow$ **if** \<expr\> **then** \<openstmt\> **else** \<closedstmt\>

25.   Show that the order in which LR(1) states are merged when optimizing LR(1) parsers can make a difference. That is, if states are merged in one order, the size of the optimized LR(1) machine may be greater than if some other order is chosen.

Ans: Consider the following grammar:

S	$\longrightarrow$	gBc
	$\longrightarrow$	gAf
	$\longrightarrow$	hBd
	$\longrightarrow$	hAf
	$\longrightarrow$	lBc
	$\longrightarrow$	lBd
	$\longrightarrow$	lAf
	$\longrightarrow$	kAd
	$\longrightarrow$	kBe
	$\longrightarrow$	mAc
	$\longrightarrow$	mBe
B	$\longrightarrow$	a
A	$\longrightarrow$	a

Among the LR(1) states generated by this grammar, there are five states with the same core:

| State 1: | B | $\rightarrow$ | $a \bullet, \{c\}$ |
| | A | $\rightarrow$ | $a \bullet, \{f\}$ |

| State 2: | B | $\rightarrow$ | $a \bullet, \{d\}$ |
| | A | $\rightarrow$ | $a \bullet, \{f\}$ |

| State 3: | B | $\rightarrow$ | $a \bullet, \{c,d\}$ |
| | A | $\rightarrow$ | $a \bullet, \{f\}$ |

| State 4: | B | $\rightarrow$ | $a \bullet, \{e\}$ |
| | A | $\rightarrow$ | $a \bullet, \{d\}$ |

| State 5: | B | $\rightarrow$ | $a \bullet, \{e\}$ |
| | A | $\rightarrow$ | $a \bullet, \{c\}$ |

Here are two legal ways of collapsing these states. Neither of these alternatives permit further collapsing, but the number of states in the result is not the same in both cases.

Alternative One: {123} {45}
Alternative Two: {14} {25} {3}

26. Show that if the basis items of an LR(1) state are weakly compatible, then all the items in that state must be weakly compatible.

Ans: It is not difficult to establish that two states are weakly compatible if and only if their basis sets are weakly compatible. This fact is handy in that it makes checking for weak compatibility easier: only basis configurations need be checked (pairwise) for conditions 1, 2, and 3. To prove this result, we assume that it is possible for two states *not* to be weakly compatible, while their basis sets are. We show this assumption leads to a contradiction.

Assume configurations C_1 and C_2 in state s, and configurations $\overline{C}_1$ and $\overline{C}_2$ in state $\overline{s}$ fail to satisfy the weak compatibility conditions. That is, $b \in L_1 \cap \overline{L}_2$, and $L_1 \cap L_2 = \phi$, and $\overline{L}_1 \cap \overline{L}_2 = \phi$, where L_i is the lookahead set corresponding to C_i. At least one of C_1 and C_2 must be a closure configuration. With out loss of generality we may assume C_1 is a closure configuration. If b were a spontaneous lookahead (that is arising from the basis item's core, not propagated by the closure operation from the basis item's lookahead), or if b were propagated from a spontaneous lookahead, then b would appear in both L_1 and $\overline{L}_1$. But then we would have $\overline{L}_1 \cap \overline{L}_2 \neq \phi$, a contradiction. Therefore b must be propagated from a basis item, which we will call C_3. In other words, $b \in L_3$.

$\overline{C}_2$ is either a basis or a closure item.

Suppose $\overline{C}_2$ is a basis item. One of our assumptions is that $b \in L_1 \cap \overline{L}_2$, so we can conclude that $b \in L_3 \cap \overline{L}_2$. Notice, if b is propagated from C_3 to C_1, then all lookaheads from C_3 are propagated to C_1, that is, $L_3 \subset L_1$. So, $L_1 \cap L_2 = \phi \Rightarrow L_3 \cap L_2 = \phi$. But we have $L_1 \cap L_2 = \phi$ by assumption. Propagating the lookahead of the basis configurations is a characteristic of the core of the basis configuration, not of the basis configuration's lookahead. So, similarly, we may conclude that $\overline{L}_3 \cap \overline{L}_2 = \phi$. Putting these together we have $b \in L_3 \cap \overline{L}_2$ and $L_3 \cap L_2 = \phi$ and $\overline{L}_3 \cap \overline{L}_2 = \phi$, which implies that basis(s) and basis($\bar{s}$) are weakly incompatible, a contradiction.

If, on the other hand, $\bar{C}_2$ is a closure item, then b must be propagated from some basis item $\bar{C}_4$, because, if b were spontaneous, then $b \in L_2$ would hold, which would imply $L_1 \cap L_2 \neq \phi$, a contradiction. By repeating the argument of the preceding paragraph reading L_4 for L_2, we may conclude $b \in L_3 \cap \bar{L}_4$ and $L_3 \cap \bar{L}_4 = \phi$ and $\bar{L}_3 \cap \bar{L}_4 = \phi$. Once again, this implies that basis(s) and basis($\bar{s}$) are weakly incompatible, a contradiction.

Thus, weak compatibility of a pair of states follows from the weak compatibility of the corresponding basis sets.

27. Show that any LL(1) grammar without λ-productions is LR(0).

Ans: In exercise 5 it is established that, so long as there are no non-terminals that generate only λ, an LL(1) grammar generates a CFSM with one basis item per state. Notice that only a basis item can signal a reduce action, since there are no λ-productions. To see that there also cannot be an action conflict in any state, suppose the basis item of some state signals a reduction. Observe that there can be no other items in the state.

28. Show that there exist LR(0) grammars, SLR(1) grammars and LALR(1) grammars that are not LL(1).

Ans:

$$
\begin{aligned}
S &\rightarrow ab \\
S &\rightarrow ac
\end{aligned}
$$

31. Show that all LL(1) grammars are also LR(1).

Ans: Lemma. Assume the grammar G is LL(1). Given any state in the LR(1) machine for G, if $A \rightarrow \gamma \bullet \alpha, a$ and $B \rightarrow \delta \bullet \beta, b$ are distinct basis items in that state, then $\text{First}(\alpha a) \cap \text{First}(\beta b) = \phi$.

This lemma rules out the possibility of shift-reduce and reduce-reduce conflicts where the items in conflict are each in the closure of distinct basis items. If a conflict were to occur among the closure of a single basis item, G would not be LL(1). There would either be left recursion in the grammar or intersecting Predict sets for two productions with the same left-hand sides. So the lemma implies the desired result.

We show the lemma holds by induction on the length of the shortest path from the initial state. Since there is only one basis item in the initial state, the basis of our induction is trivial. We sketch the induction step in which we use the induction assumption that the current state satisfies the property to show that (immediate) successor states must also satisfy the property.

Any pair of basis items in the successor state must come from two items of the current state that are shifted on the same symbol. We consider two cases.

If the two items in the current state are each in the closure of distinct basis items, then the induction hypothesis entails that the symbol that shifts these two items must be a non-terminal that derives only λ. Otherwise, the First sets of the distinct basis items would intersect. The First sets of the two items that shift to the same successor state are unchanged by shifting the λ non-terminal. Furthermore, closure items have smaller First sets than do the basis items in whose closure they live. Putting these two observations together with the induction assumption, we may conclude that the two basis items in the successor state must have disjoint First sets.

If the two items in the current state are in the closure of the same basis item, then one of three subcases must hold. First, if the two items are on a path in the 'requires the addition of' graph (See the solution to exercise 5), then there is a left recursion. Second, if the two items are not on a path and are shifted on a symbol X such that $First(X)$ is not $\{\lambda\}$, then there must be a pair of productions with intersecting Predict sets and the same left-hand side (Again, see the solution to exercise 5). Third, if the two items are not on a path and are shifted on a symbol X such that $First(X)$ is $\{\lambda\}$, then the First sets of the corresponding basis items in the successor state are the same as the First sets of the items before the shift. So if these First sets are not disjoint, there must again be a pair of productions with intersecting Predict sets and the same left-hand side. So, only the third subcase is possible, and in it we have shown by contradiction that the basis items in the successor state must have disjoint First sets. This completes the proof.

35.   Consider the follow grammar that has $O(n^2)$ productions:

$$S \longrightarrow X_i\, z_i \qquad 1 \le i \le n$$
$$X_i \longrightarrow y_j\, X_i \mid y_j \qquad 1 \le i,j \le n, i \ne j$$

Show that the CFSM for this grammar has $O(2^n)$ states. Is the grammar SLR(1)?

Ans: All states besides the initial state have basis item sets of the form $\{X_i \longrightarrow y_k \bullet X_i \mid i \in R\}$ for some $R \subset \{1,2,...,n\}$, and some k. Intuitively, R is the set of indices that have not subscripted any of the y_i's shifted so far. That can be any subset of $\{1,2,...,n\}$, so there are $O(2^n)$ states.

The grammar is SLR because the Follow sets for the X_i's, $\{z_i\}$, are disjoint, and none of those Follow sets intersect any of the $First(X_j)$'s. Thus, Follow sets used as lookaheads are sufficient to resolve all potential conflicts.

6.5. Chapter 7 Solutions

1. The discussion of syntax-directed translation in Section 7.1 depends on the assumption that an
    abstract syntax tree can be constructed from the sequence of parse actions generated by a parser as it
    parses a program. An abstract syntax tree is not a literal parse tree, but it contains the "semantically
    useful" details of the corresponding parse tree.

    (a) Give an algorithm for constructing a *parse tree* from the sequence of actions generated by an
         LL or LR parser.

Ans: The following algorithms use an auxiliary stack, TreeStack, to build up parse trees for both LL and
        LR parsers. The function MakeLeafNode is for constructing a TreeNode without branches, where
        function MakeTreeNode is used to construct a TreeNode with its first argument as the label and
        other arguments as the (ordered) branches. (See Section 14.2 for a possible definition of the inter-
        face to this kind of tree representations).

```
        — an auxiliary stack for building up parse trees
        TreeStack : Stack of TreeNode;

        — from LR parse actions to parse trees
        function Build_LR_ParseTree(actions : in Sequence of LR_ParseAction)
            return TreeNode is
        action : LR_ParseAction;
    begin
        TreeStack := EmptyStack;
        action := first(actions);      — get the first action in sequence
        while action /= accept loop
            if action = shift on symbol a then
                Push(TreeStack, MakeLeafNode(a));
            else — action = reduce by p : A —> A₁A₂ · · · Aₙ
                Pop top n nodes from TreeStack as C₁C₂ · · · Cₙ;
                    — assuming C₁ is the top node (i.e. last Pushed)
                Push(TreeStack, MakeTree(A, Cₙ, ..., C₁));
                    — Note the reverse order here
            end if;
            action := next(actions);    — get the next action in sequence
        end loop;
        return Top(TreeStack); — there should be only one node left on the stack
    end Build_LR_ParseTree;
```

— from LL parse actions to parse trees
— in this case we augment each production by an end-of-production
— symbol (EOP), and the LL parse actions are augmented by an action
— "end of production p". The LL parsers need necessary changes
— to generate proper actions.

```
function Build_LL_ParseTree(actions : in Sequence of LL_ParseAction)
      return TreeNode is
   action : LL_ParseAction;
begin
   TreeStack := EmptyStack;
   action := first(actions);      — get the first action in sequence
   while action /= accept loop
      if action = match symbol a then
        Push(TreeStack, MakeLeafNode(a));
      elsif action = end of production p then
         — assuming p = A —> A₁A₂ · · · Aₙ, n ≥ 0
         Pop top n nodes from TreeStack as C₁C₂ · · · Cₙ;
         Push(TreeStack, MakeTree(A, Cₙ, ..., C₁));
      else — action = predict production p
        — the LL parser should push an EOP symbol (with its associated
        — production number) onto the "parse stack" before the right-hand
        — side symbols are pushed.
        Do Nothing;               — nothing is done here
      end if;
      action := next(actions);     — get the next action in sequence
   end loop;
   return Top(TreeStack); — there should be only one node left on the stack
end Build_LL_ParseTree;
```

As can be seen from the above, the construction of parse trees from LR parse actions is rather straightforward. It is a little more complicated for the LL case.

(b)   Explain how this algorithm would have to be changed to produce an *abstract syntax tree* instead.

Ans: Abstract syntax trees can be constructed much as parse trees are, but with following changes:

(1)   Each terminal symbol is marked as (semantically) significant or insignificant. Only significant terminal symbols are pushed onto TreeStack. Examples of significant terminal symbols are identifiers and numeric literals. Examples of insignificant terminal symbols are reserved words and punctuation. In general, we consider a significant symbol to be either a nonterminal symbol or a significant terminal symbol.

(2)   Each production is associated with the number of significant symbols in it. When a production is reduced (the LR case) or the end of production is reached (the LL case), only this number of nodes are popped from TreeStack.

(3)   Each nonleaf node is labeled by a production number instead of a nonterminal symbol. This is needed because we may have two different productions of the same nonterminal to have the same significant symbols on their right-hand sides. Using nonterminal symbols as the labels can't distinguish them in this case.

(4)   If a production has only one significant symbol on its right-hand side, and no other production with the same left-hand side nonterminal has the same right-hand side significant symbol, then when the production is reduced, no action is needed on TreeStack. An example of this case is:

<primary>   —> (<expression>)

Note that the abstract syntax trees constructed in this way might not be what the user really wanted. This is particularly true for the LL case: Since no left recursion is allowed in LL grammars, left associative expressions can hardly be constructed correctly. Using action routines to explicitly construct abstract syntax trees has more control on the final shape of the trees.

3.   The discussion of semantic error handling in Section 7.2.3 described standard actions to be taken by every semantic routine to deal with the possibility that one or more of its inputs might be an Error record. Outline an algorithm for a code preprocessor that would take as input a semantic routine without error handling code and would add the appropriate code to handle Error records.

Ans: Given a semantic routine R with **in** parameters $a_1, a_2, ..., a_i$, **out** parameters $b_1, b_2, ..., b_j$, and **in out** parameters $c_1, c_2, ..., c_k$. The code preprocessor could just add the following statement as the first statement to R:

```
if a₁ = Error or  · · · aᵢ = Error or
   c₁ = Error or  · · · cₖ = Error
then
   b₁ := Error; · · · bⱼ := Error;
   c₁ := Error; · · · cₖ := Error;
   return;
end if;
```

In this way, each transformed semantic routine would check and propagate Error records as its first action.

4.   One distinct disadvantage of implementing a semantic stack as an array is the possibility of stack overflow due to the fixed size of the array. Despite this disadvantage, arrays are used more often than linked lists for semantic stack implementation because of the simplicity of implementing a stack with an array and because the Push and Pop operations are more efficient than using a list of dynamically allocated semantic records. Design an alternative semantic stack implementation that handles stacks of any number of elements but is close to the efficiency of an array as long as the number of records on the stack stays below some fixed number. Analytically or empirically compare the performance of your implementation to that of an array implementation.

Ans: We could use a linked list of fixed-size array segments for implementing a semantic stack. Then as long as Push and Pop operations do not cause overflow or underflow of an array segment, the only efficiency penalty will be the extra level of indirection for accessing current array segment. Even that can be avoided if we always keep the top segment in a static array, and are willing to do more work for copying an array segment to/from the static array when underflow/overflow occurs. In either case, we get an implementation of semantic stack that is close to the efficiency of a fixed-array implementation as long as the number of records on the stack stays below the size of an array segment.

5. Add an if statement production like the one in Section 7.1.3 to the parser-controlled stack grammar for Micro in Figure 7.10. The following information should be used as a basis for parameterizing the action symbols:

- The StartIf action routine requires the semantic record associated with <expression> as input and leaves information in the semantic record associated with **then**.

- FinishIf uses the output of StartIf as input and produces no semantic record.

Also add an if statement production that includes an else part. A new action routine will have to be introduced that uses the output of StartIf as input and leaves its output for FinishIf.

Ans:

(a)   <statement> $\longrightarrow$ **if** <expression> #StartIf($2,$3) **then**
                                    <statement list> **end if** #FinishIf($3)

(b)   <statement> $\longrightarrow$ **if** <expression> #StartIf($2,$5) **then**
                                    <statement list> <else part> **end if** #FinishIf($5)
       <else part> $\longrightarrow$ **else** #ProcessElse($$) <statement list>
       <else part> $\longrightarrow \lambda$

Where the new semantic routine ProcessElse uses the output of StartIf as input and leaves its output at the same place for FinishIf.

6. Design an algorithm to rewrite productions with internal action symbols to make them usable by an LR parser. (See Section 7.2.2).

Ans: Given a grammar G consisting of productions with internal action symbols, we do the following:

For each production p of G with internal action symbol a,

   p: <nonterminal N> $\longrightarrow$ ... #a ...

We add a new nonterminal <production p action a> and new production p′

   p′: <production p action a> $\longrightarrow \lambda$ #a

to G. Then we rewrite production p into

   p: <nonterminal N> $\longrightarrow$ ... <production p action a> ...

with action symbol #a being replaced by the nonterminal <production p action a>. The transformed grammar G′ will be equivalent to the original grammar G, but the action symbols only appear at the end of each production, hence directly usable by an LR parser.

8.   Translate the program from exercise 7 into postfix, triples and tuples, as in Section 7.3.2.

Ans: (postfix)

A 5 := ; B A 2 − := ; C 1 A B + − := ; **end**

(triples)

(1) (:= 5 A)
(2) (− A 2)
(3) (:= (2) B)
(4) (+ A B)
(5) (− 1 (4))
(6) (:= (5) C)

(tuples)

(:= 5 A)
(− A 2 T1)
(:= T1 B)
(+ A B T2)
(− 1 T2 T3)
(= T3 C)

6.6. Chapter 8 Solutions

1.   The two data structures most commonly used to implement symbol tables in production compilers are binary search trees and hash tables. What are the advantages and disadvantages of each of these data structures?

Ans: (a) Binary Trees

Advantages:

- The amount of space used by a binary tree is proportional to the actual number of entries in it. In cases where many small symbol tables are maintained at the same time, as in the one symbol table per scope approach, this means a more space-economical choice.

- If the tree is always kept balanced, the worst case cost for a look up is $O(\log n)$, independent of the distribution of the actual name patterns.

- It's very easy to get a *sorted* list of all the entries in a binary tree, which means no extra work is needed in, for example, producing a cross reference map for a program.

Disadvantages:

- If the binary tree is not kept balanced, the worst case look up could be as costly as linear search. However, if the tree is kept balanced, each insertion operation may need extra work to adjust the tree.

- New entries are added at the frontier of a tree, hence it is harder to implement the single global symbol table approach using binary trees. (see. p. 264, Section 8.3)

(b) Hash Tables

Advantages:

- The average case look up cost can be very good, approaching $O(1)$, if the hash function and key distribution are uniform and the table is not very densely occupied.

- For the chained resolution implementation, new entries are naturally added at the front of the chains. Hence it is easier to implement the single global symbol table organization.

Disadvantages:

- There is usually a fixed (maybe large) space overhead in addition to the space required for storing actual entries. Hence less attractive for implementing the one symbol table per scope approach.

- The worst case cost for look up could be of $O(n)$, i.e. as in linear search. Although this is not very likely to happen in any reasonable implementation and common key distribution.

- Explicit sorting is needed to produce an ordered list of entries in a hash table.

2.   If a hash table is being used in a situation where dynamic storage allocation is not practical, external collision resolution may be implemented by allocating entries on the hash chains from a fixed array.

Compare this approach to internal resolution techniques and to external chaining with dynamic allocation to determine its strengths and weaknesses.

Ans: The approach of resolving external collision by hash chains from a fixed array can be viewed as a compromise between internal resolution and external chaining with dynamic allocation. It has most of the advantages of external chaining with dynamic allocation approach, *if* the pre-allocated, fixed, array is used properly and effectively. However, since the fixed array is playing the role of a heap in the dynamic allocation approach, we need to write our own version of memory manager in order to use the array effectively (e.g. be able to share and reuse the space of the array). That is by no means a piece of trivial code. Also, it is rather difficult to determine the proper size of the fixed array that works well in all cases.

5.   For what languages is use a string space representation of identifiers inappropriate? Why?

Ans: Many older languages, such as Basic or Fortran (II, IV), only allow identifiers to have some fixed maximum length (and generally quite short, such as 4 or 6). For those languages, the extra space and time overhead imposed by the string space approach may not be worthwhile and the naive approach of storing the identifiers directly in their associated symbol table entries may just do well.

6.   Compare the two approaches to handling the names of record fields. How well does each work with each of the multiple scope alternatives?

Ans: The approach that uses one symbol table for each record type localizes all the fields of a record in one place. It fits particularly well with the one symbol table per scope approach because a record type essentially creates a new scope for its fields, and a single look up mechanism can handle both cases. The record number approach fits more pleasantly with the global symbol table scheme because no other symbol table is created, and a slightly modified look up mechanism can handle both fields and ordinary names. (See Section 8.4.1, Fields and Records, for more details)

7.   Describe the handling of names exported by a Modula-2 module (as presented in Section 8.4.2) to a surrounding scope for each of the two multiple scope alternatives.

Ans: For individual symbol table (per scope) approach, the entries of the *exported* names are *moved* to the symbol table of the surrounding scope when the exporting scope is closed. Whereas for the single global symbol table approach, when the exporting scope is closed, all entries of the *nonexported* names are *removed* from the global symbol table, which effectively keeps only the exported entries in the surrounding scope.

8.   Compare the two approaches to handling imported names. How well does each work with each of the two scope representation alternatives?

Ans: The approach that creates a new copy of the imported entries in the current scope works well in either of the scope representation alternatives (i.e. using individual symbol table or a global symbol table). The approach of using a maximum depth field seems to fit better with the single global symbol table representation because it is easier in this case to find all symbols that must have their maximum depth field reset when a scope in which an import was done is closed. (See Section 8.4.3, Import Rules, for more details)

11. The concept of perfect hashing was introduced in Section 3.5 as a method for fast recognition of key-words by a scanner. Many of the articles published on this topic have stressed algorithms to create *minimal* perfect hash tables so as to use as little space as possible. One drawback to such an approach is that most or all of the strings for non-keyword identifiers will produce hash values that collide with keyword hash values, thus requiring a string comparison to make the final decision about the token. Since string comparisons are slow on many machines, we would rather avoid them. A larger hash table would allow some hash values to have no associated keyword. If an identifier maps to such a value, no string comparison is required in order to make the identifier/keyword decision. Study the relationship between hash table size for perfect hash functions and keyword recognition efficiency either experimentally of analytically.

Ans: Actually, in many cases, we could have a "minimal" perfect hash table but use larger hash value domain to get similar effect of using a larger and sparser hash table. For example, we could use a mapping function m, which maps each character to an integer. The mapping m is designed with the property that the hash function used, say h(ID) = m(first_char(ID)) + m(last_char(ID)), produces hash values in the range of say, 10 .. 158, but for all reserved words their hash values lie within 17 .. 56. Now only identifiers which are also hashed into the range of the reserved words need to do string comparisons.

In theory, it may require exponential time to find such a mapping function m (by trying out all possi-ble mappings from characters to some fixed range of integers) for a particular set of keywords. However, in many practical cases (such as the reserved words for Algol 60 or Pascal), the search time turns out to be quite reasonable.

12. In the discussion of record field names in Section 8.4.1, we mentioned that some languages allow abbreviations of the expressions for naming fields. Using the example in that section, R.X.C and R.C would be equivalent references as would R.X.A and R.A. Describe necessary data structures and an algorithm for correctly handling such field references.

Ans: Basically, we can resolve the abbreviated field names by either top-down or bottom-up approach, somewhat similar to the two alternatives of overloading resolution to be discussed in Section 11.3.7. For one-pass, left-to-right compiling, it may be more natural to use top-down approach in this case.

Assuming the standard PL/1 resolution rules are used, i.e.,
(1) If the reference fully qualifies a field, then it names that field.
(2) Otherwise the abbreviated reference must *uniquely* qualify some field.

To do top-down resolution, we need to be able to access all the fields of a record type. For example, we could associate with each record type entry in the symbol table a linked list of entries for its immediate fields. Or if we implemented a record type using a binary tree for its fields, the same tree could serve our purpose.

Let us define some types and auxiliary functions first:

type ST_Entry = SymbolTableEntryType;   — defined elsewhere

type Access_Path = List **of** ST_Entry;
— Each Access_Path is used to "fully" specify the access path from a
— record to some field of it or of its fields or its fields' fields etc.
— We use "names" in writing out Access_Paths, but they actually mean their
— corresponding symbol table (attributes) entries.

function Records_With_Field_Name(Recs: List **of** Access_Path; N : Name)
                return List **of** Access_Path;
— For each element of "Recs", say <A, ..., X>, if it fully names a
— record R, and R has a field entry, say Y, named "N", then append
— Y to the original Access_Path and put it (i.e. <A, ..., X, Y>) in the
— result list.

function Fields_Of_Records(Recs : List **of** Access_Path)
                return List **of** Access_Path;
— For each element of "Recs", say <A, ..., K>, if it fully names a
— record R, and R has fields S, T, ..., X, then add Access_Paths
— <A, ..., K, S>, <A, ..., K, T>, ..., <A, ..., K, X> to the
— result list.

function Lookup_All(N : Name) **return** List **of** Access_Path;
— returns a list of access paths, where each one identifies a different
— entry named "N" by looking up the symbol table of current scope.

function Append_AP_List(L1, L2: List **of** Access_Path)
                return List **of** Access_Path;
— append two lists and return the result

Now we define the main procedures for doing abbreviation resolution:

— NL is the list of input names (e.g. A.B....N becomes <A, B, ..., N>).
— We don't have to collect the list of names then do resolution, but
— to simplify the presentation of the algorithm, we use this explicit
— argument for the list of names.

— In the following "first" takes the first element of a list, "rest"
— returns a new list of the argument list with first element removed.

```
procedure Resolve_Abbrev(NL: in List of Name;
                 result: out Access_Path; unique: out Boolean) is
   possible_results : List of Access_Path;
begin
     — we look up the ST_Entry for the first name of the list NL,
     — then collect all possible references by calling the function
     — Find_Qualified_Fields as defined below.
     possible_results := Find_Qualified_Fields(
                       Lookup_All(first(NL)),
                       rest(NL));
     if possible_results = null then
         — Error "No qualified field"
         unique := false;
     elsif length(possible_results) = 1 then
         result := first(possible_results);
         unique := true;
     elsif there is an entry R which is fully qualified by NL
           — this can be easily checked by comparing the length of R with
           — the length of NL
         result := R;
         unique := true;
      else
         — Error "Ambiguous abbreviation"
         unique := false;
      end if;
end Resolve_Abbrev;

function Find_Qualified_Fields(AL: List of Access_Path; NL: List of Name)
                 return List of Access_Path is
begin
    if NL = null then
        return AL;
    elsif AL = null then
        return null;
    else
        return Append_AP_List(
                Find_Qualified_Fields(Records_With_Field_Name(AL, first(NL)),
                         rest(NL)),
                Find_Qualified_Fields(Fields_Of_Records(AL), NL));
    end if
end Find_Qualified_Fields;
```

13. Another way of naming record fields is in the opposite order as is used in Pascal, Ada and similar languages. That is, C.X.R would be used instead of R.X.C. Describe necessary data structures and an algorithm for correctly handling such field references in a single left-to-right pass.

Ans: In this case it is more natural to use bottom-up resolution algorithm. The approach is very similar to the one given above for Exercise 12. However, instead of linking a record type to all its fields as was required in Exercise 12, here we need to link each field to its defining (parent) record type. For this exercise, we assume that the field names are given in the opposite order but in *full,* that is, there is no abbreviation of fields as in Exercise 12.

First we need some type definitions and auxiliary functions similar to the ones given for Exercise 12.

```
                — The same definitions
                type ST_Entry ...
                type Access_Path ...
                function Lookup_All ...

                function Records_Of_Name(Recs: List of Access_Path; N : Name)
                            return List of Access_Path;
                — For each element of "Recs", say <R, S, ...>, if R is a record entry
                — and its name is "N", then put <R, S, ...> in the result list.

                function Records_Of_Fields(Flds: List of Access_Path) : List of Access_Path;
                — For each element of "Flds", say <S, T, ...>, if S is a field of some
                — record R, then add <R, S, T, ...> to the result list.

                — See comments for Exercise 12, procedure Resolve_Abbrev.
                procedure Resolve_Opposite(NL: in List of Name;
                                    result: out Access_Path;
                                    unique: out Boolean) is
                  possible_results : List of Access_Path;
                begin
                    possible_results := Find_Qualified_Records(Lookup_All(first(NL)),
                                        rest(NL));
                    if possible_results = null then
                        — Error "No qualified record was found"
                        unique := false;
                    elsif length(possible_results) = 1 and
                        it's of the same length of NL then   — since no abbrev is allowed
                        result := first(possible_results);
                        unique := true;
                    else
                        — Error "Not fully qualified reference"
                        unique := false;
                    end if;
                end Resolve_Opposite;

                function Find_Qualified_Records(AL: List of Access_Path; NL: List of Name)
                            return List of Access_Path is
                begin
                    if NL = null then
                        return AL;
                    elsif AL = null then
                        return null;
                    else
                        return Find_Qualified_Records(
                                Records_Of_Name(Records_Of_Fields(AL), first(NL)),
                                rest(NL));
                    end if;
                end Find_Qualified_Records;
```

Note that since we assume that abbreviations of the expressions for naming fields are not allowed in this case, the algorithm is somewhat simpler than that of exercise 12. Also, since the elements of parameter NL are not reused in Find_Qualified_Records (cf. the procedure Find_Qualified_Fields in Exercise 12), NL could be made implicit more easily in this case (e.g. by calling to scanner directly for next name where it is needed).

14.   How would the altered search rules described in exercises 12 and 13 affect the implementation of **with** statements in Pascal?

Ans: For the case of abbreviated field references, the first "Lookup_All" will have to take into account all the records that have been opened by the enclosing **with** statements at current point (or all record scopes on the current scope stack). Also, the way to check for fully qualified references will have to be modified because we can no longer simply compare the length of the access path to the length of the names for this checking. Instead we may want, for example, to keep a flag along with each access path which says if this path is fully qualified by the names or could be abbreviated by the names.

As for the case of using opposite field names, we need to check the possible results against the **with** scope stack. Any access path that can be "grafted" to the records opened by the enclosing **with** statements must be considered as a plausible answer.

That is, in either case the procedure Resolve_... would need some changes to either start with extra work and/or do extra work in checking the returned results. One thing we must be careful about in making the changes is that since the ordering of **with** statements is important, we must resolve the final possible results in the same order of the opened records.

6.7. Chapter 9 Solutions

1. Programming languages provide constructors for a variety of data objects. Suggest the run-time storage organization most appropriate for each of the classes of data objects described below:

    list of T;

    T is any type name. Lists may be catenated using an **append** operation, and decomposed using **head** and **tail** operations.

    Ans: Lists are naturally implemented by a linked structure of dynamically allocated nodes. They can be defined as follows:

    list of T = **null** (for representing the empty list) or
                 access List_Cell(T)

    where

         List_Cell(T) = **record**
                             item : T;
                             next : **access** List_Cell;
                         end record;

    and T is a generic type parameter.

    set of Lower .. Upper;

    Lower and Upper are constant values. This is essentially the set constructor provided in Pascal.

    Ans: Sets of enumeration types can be implemented as boolean (characteristic) vectors, for example,

         set of Lower .. Upper = **array** [Lower .. Upper] **of** Boolean;

    For better space efficiency, we can use more compact form, such as bit vectors, to represent the boolean arrays.

    set of Lower .. Upper;

    Lower and Upper are expressions evaluated at run-time when the set declaration is elaborated.

    Ans: The dope vector approach for handling dynamic arrays can be used here for implementing sets with dynamic bounds. That is, they are represented as boolean arrays with dynamic bounds.

    set of T;

    T is any type name.

    Ans: Structures used for implementing symbol tables, such as linear lists, binary trees, and hash tables, could be used to represent sets of any type.

ExtendedInt;

ExtendedInt is an extended precision integer. There is no MaxInt or MinInt bound; rather, the precision of the representation is extended as needed to accommodate any value.

Ans: Extended precision integers can be represented as a list (or an array) of "big" digits, together with a sign flag. Each big digit could be any convenient storage unit such as a byte, a word, or a long word. E.g.

> **type** EntendedInt = **record**
> > sign: (positive, zero, negative);
> > magnitude: **list of** bigdigit;
> > **end record**;

file of T;

T is any type except a file (or a structure that contains a file). This is the file constructor provided in Pascal.

Ans: This could be implemented by some kind of file descriptor record such as:

> **file of** T = **record**
> > fp: File_Pointer_Type;   — operating system dependent
> > item_size: Integer;   — size of T
> > — following fields may be optional,
> > — depending on what is in fp^
> > current_position: Integer; — where to read/write
> > buffer: T;   — current item under read/write head
> > mode: (readonly, writeonly, readwrite);
> > status: (Error, Eof, Normal);
> > **end record**;

String(N);

N is a constant value. The string may vary in length from 0 to N.

Ans: Strings with fixed maximum length can be organized as an array (of fixed size) of characters together with its current length. For example,

> **type** String(N) = **record**
> > current_length: 0 .. N;
> > text: **array** [1 .. N] **of** Character;
> > **end record**;

String(N);

N is an expression evaluated at run-time when the string declaration is elaborated. The string may vary in length from 0 to N. This is essentially the string constructor provided in PL/I.

Ans: Instead of allocating a fixed-size array as part of the record, for strings with *fixed* but *dynamic* bound we must keep their maximum length and a pointer to the dynamically allocated text array in the string descriptors. Type definitions such as the following can be used in this case.

type String(N) = **record**
                    maximum_length: Integer; — filled in at elaboration time
                    current_length: Integer; — check for 0 .. N at run time
                    text: **access array** [1 .. N] of Character;
                    — the actual array is allocated at elaboration time
        end record;

The string texts may be allocated either on the stack or from heap, depending of the semantics of the languages and other implementation decisions.

5.   On some computers it is possible to extend the maximum accessible memory address, thereby increasing the effective size of memory. This memory extension operation could be valuable when a program has exhausted free memory because of the growth of dynamic memory structures. How would you lay out a program in memory to allow for possible expansion?

Ans: A possible layout could be:

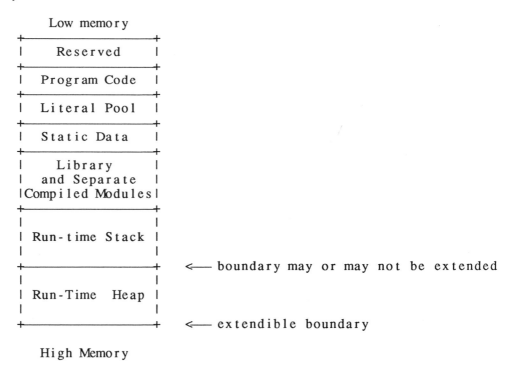

6.   The handshaking scheme presented in Section 9.3.3 for recognizing accessible heap objects does not safely allow heap compaction. Suggest a generalization of the scheme that does allow compaction. Hint: Generalize the two-way handshake into a three-way handshake.

Ans: We generalize the two-way handshake into a three-way handshake by introducing one more level of indirection, as shown in the following figure: (using strings as an example)

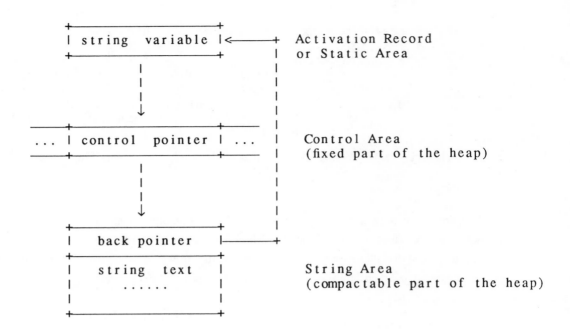

Using this scheme, an accessible heap object is recognized (during a garbage collection) by following its back pointer to the string variable and then to the control pointer and finally back to the same heap object. Any heap object with a broken chain of pointers can be safely collected. Now when an accessible heap object is moved (for compaction), we follow the above chain and update its control pointer to point to the new address, whereas the associated string variable itself is not changed at all.

The control area can be dynamically allocated from the heap or statically allocated, the only important thing is that it must not be directly accessible to user programs. As one can see, the control pointers themselves are not movable in the control area. This should not impose any problem however, because control pointers are fixed-size objects and no compaction is necessary for reusing freed space. The allocation of control pointers can either use a bitmap approach, or keep a free list of all unused slots.

7.   Many compilers allocate a fixed set of registers for use as display registers. In some cases this policy may overallocate registers to the display, wasting them. In other cases the display may be too small, limiting the class of programs that can be successfully compiled.

Outline an algorithm that a compiler might use to determine the exact number of display registers needed for a particular program. What problems arise if this algorithm is used in a one-pass compiler?

Ans: A very simple algorithm that keeps track of the "high-water" mark of the nesting levels of a program will serve our purpose. For example, the compiler could define an integer variable max_display, with initial value 0, whenever it starts compiling a procedure (or block) at i'th nesting level it will set max_display to i if the value of i is greater than the current value of max_display.

Unfortunately, this algorithm doesn't work well in a one-pass compiler. This is because the final value of max_display won't be known until all the procedures (blocks) are seen, which means it won't be known until the whole program is compiled in a one-pass compiler. Because the code generation module needs to know how many display registers are available for it to generate proper code along the way in a one-pass compiler, a problem arises: In order to generate code we need to know the final value of max_display; in order to know the final value of max_display, we need to compile (hence generate code for) the whole program.

8. Assume we organize a heap so that only one pointer to any heap object is allowed. What operations must be done when a pointer to a heap object is over-written? What operations must be done when a scope is opened and closed? Can assignment of pointers or heap objects be allowed?

Ans:

(a) When a pointer to a heap object is overwritten, the object whose sole reference is being destroyed must be deallocated. This may be done explicitly by returning it to the free list, or it can be delayed until garbage collection time.

(b) When a scope is opened, all pointer variables in the AR just created must be initialized to null, so that no garbage will be accidently taken as meaningful heap object. When a scope is closed, all heap objects pointed to by the pointer variables in the AR to be popped must be deallocated as in (a).

(c) Assignment of pointers is not allowed in this case, but assignment of heap objects can be allowed if the semantics of the assignment is to make a new "copy" of the heap object and assign the pointer to the new copy to the pointer variable being assigned.

9. Assume we organize a heap using reference counts. What operations must be done when a pointer to a heap object is assigned? What operations must be done when a scope is opened and closed?

Ans:

(a) When a pointer to a heap object is assigned to some variable, the reference count of the heap object pointed by the *old* value (which is a pointer) of the variable is decremented by one, and if the count reaches zero, the object is freed. Also, the reference count of the heap object to be assigned to the variable is incremented by one.

(b) When a scope is opened, all pointer variables in the AR just created must be initialized to null. When a scope is closed, all heap objects pointed by the pointer variables in the AR to be popped must have their reference counts decremented by one and freed if necessary as in (a).

10. Some languages, including C, contain an operation that creates a pointer to a data object. That is,

P := Adr(X);

would take the address of object X whose type is T, and assign it to p whose type is $\uparrow$T.

How is management of the run-time stack complicated if it is possible to create pointers to arbitrary data objects in activation records?

What restrictions on the creation and copying of pointers to data objects suffice to guarantee the integrity of the run-time stack?

Ans:

(a)   Since the conventional way of managing run-time a stack is to deallocate (destroy) all data objects in an activation record when a subprogram returns to its caller, allowing pointers to arbitrary data objects in activation records will certainly create the so-called "dangling" pointer problem. This problem can be avoided by retaining activation records even after the calls have returned, but then we essentially lose the "stack" discipline. Alternatively, we might move those "pointed to" objects to the heap and update their pointers. This could be a very expensive operation, if not wholly impossible. A more practical solution is to impose some syntactic restrictions as given below.

(b)   To guarantee the integrity of the run-time stack, we might require that the "life-time" of a "pointed to" object be at least that of its referencing pointer variable. The following restrictions suffice to guarantee this. First, when a stack pointer is created by say,

P := Adr(X);

P's scope should not be greater than X's. Moreover, once a stack pointer is created by the Adr operation, it may not be copied to a containing scope, and it may never be returned as function's value or through an **out/in out** parameters.

11.   Assume that rather than maintaining a single heap we maintain a distinct "sub-heap" for each type T that may be dynamically allocated. What are the advantages and disadvantages of maintaining distinct sub-heaps? How do sub-heaps simplify reclamation of inaccessible heap objects?

Ans:

(a)   The advantages of maintaining distinct subheaps are: (1) Since each heap is allocated in fixed-size chunks (the size depends on the type of objects the heap is allocated for), heap management is a lot simpler and more efficient. (2) The fixed-size allocation of subheaps also means no space is wasted due to *internal* fragmentation within each subheap. The major problem with this approach is how to properly partition the global heap into subheaps. If we "statically" partition the heap, that is we pre-allocate one fixed-size subheap for each type T that may be dynamically allocated, we may run out of space in one subheap when plenty of space is still left in other subheaps. This is essentially a kind of *external* fragmentation problem. Now if we partition the heap "dynamically" on demand, then we are essentially doing "two-level" heap management, which may incur unnecessary complexity and overhead. However, some Lisp implementations use (variations of) this two-level approach for their heap management with satisfactory results.

(b)   Since objects in a subheap are always of fixed size, we can do "compaction" (which is the phase that collects and coalesces inaccessible heap objects in the garbage collection process) very easily. Any unused slot can be filled in by the object from any used slot so we don't have to move a lot of heap objects to compact the subheap. After mark-and-sweep, just scan forward from the beginning to find the "first" unused slot, then scan backward from the end to find "last" used slot, and move the last used slot to the first unused slot. The above procedure is repeated until the forward-scan pointer runs across the backward-scan pointer.

13. Some programming languages provide the following construct for the concurrent execution of program steps:

cobegin <stmt 1> | <stmt2> | $\cdots$ | <stmt n> **coend**

Each of <stmt 1>, . . . , <stmt n> can be executed concurrently or in any order. Within each statement in the cobegin construct, ordinary begin-end blocks can be used to force sequential execution.

Does an ordinary run-time stack suffice for a language that contains a **cobegin** construct? If not, how must the stack be generalized to support the concurrent or interleaved execution order allowed by the **cobegin**?

Ans: In general, a single ordinary run-time stack does not suffice for a language that contains a **cobegin** construct. We need something like *cactus stacks* (see p. 292, Section 9.2) to support the concurrent or interleaved execution introduced by the cobegin construct. There are a few ways of doing this.

First, we may allocate a separate stack segment for each concurrent statement and use static/dynamic links or display registers to set up linkages to the original "parent" stack (which is shared by all concurrent statements of a cobegin construct). The main advantage of this approach is that no penalty is paid by ordinary sequential statements and within each concurrent statement it uses its own stack segment exactly like in the situation of sequential execution. The disadvantage, which may or may not be considered important depending on the language, is that it is rather difficult to find proper stack size for each statement before execution. Smaller size means more restrictive programs, larger size means potentially wasteful use of space.

Another approach, which is on the other extreme, is to dynamically allocate activation records from the heap. Now the run-time stack effectively becomes a linked list of activation records. No special support is needed in this case to handle concurrent statements. Each concurrent statement sees its own stack as a linked list, and the run-time "stack" of the whole **cobegin** statement becomes a linked "tree." The advantage of this approach is its simplicity (if heap management is part of the standard run-time support), the disadvantage is that higher cost of allocation/deallocation of activation records are imposed on all statements. Also, a stack is usually more efficient in its reuse of space than a heap.

For interleaved execution (i.e. there is still just a single thread of control), we may use still another approach, which may or may not be more effective than the above two. In this approach, all concurrent statements share the single run-time stack, whenever one statement is "switched" to another one, we move the top part of the stack (i.e. the part created after the **cobegin** statement is executed for the statement just about to be switched) to heap, and then move the previously saved stack (if there is one) of the statement going to be executed onto the stack. This approach impose no individual limit on the stack size for each concurrent statement and when a statement is executing it sees only a single contiguous stack. The cost of moving (part of the) stack to/from heap is paid only by concurrent statements and only at statement switching time, but the cost may be a little higher.

15. Show that the display-swap approach for implementing formal procedures fails for the following Pascal program:

```
program prog(output);

procedure q;
label 1;
    procedure exec(procedure z);
    begin
        z;
    end;

    procedure r;
    begin
        goto 1;
    end;
begin
    exec(r);
1:
end;

procedure p(procedure a);
var v : integer;
begin
    v := 10;
    a;
    writeln(v);
end;

begin
    p(q);
end.
```

Does the static/dynamic chain approach handle this program correctly?

Ans: We trace the call/return sequence of executing the given program using the display-swap approach (Section 9.6.2), and get the following picture:

AR# calls/ returns	(1) prog	(2) p	(3) before calling q	(4) q	(5) exec	(6) before calling r	(7) r	(8) **goto** 1 back to q	(9) return from q to p
display	[1] ?? ? prog	[2] ?? p prog	[1] ?? ? prog	[3] ?? q prog	[4] exec q prog	[3] ?? q prog	[5] r q prog	[5] r q prog	[4] exec q prog
formal proc		a = <q,[1]>			z = <r,[3]>				
RestoreAR	???	???	(2)	(2)	(2)	(5)	(5)	(5)	(2)
saved RestoreAR			???			(2)			

As we can see from the above, after procedure r executes **goto** 1, procedure q returns to procedure p. At this point, p uses the current value of RestoreAR to restore its display registers, resulting in a wrong environment for executing p (instead of the display [2], we get display [4] as shown in the figure).

The static/dynamic chain approach does handle this program correctly, because during the life-time of an activation of a procedure, the chains associated with the activation record are never modified. No matter how you get back to a procedure, you are always in the correct environment.

6.8. Chapter 10 Solutions

1.   Outline an algorithm for testing the structural type equivalence of two types represented by TypeDescriptor records of the form defined in Figure 10.17.

Ans: Since recursive (i.e., circular) type definitions may be introduced via access types, we must be careful not to fall into infinite loops while traversing the type-descriptor structures checking for structural type equivalence. The basic idea is that whenever we see type descriptors T1 = **access** P and T2 = **access** Q, we go on and check for the equivalence of P and Q under the *assumption* that T1 and T2 are equivalent. That is, if we ever see T1 and T2 again in the course of type checking, we simply return true without tracing down their referenced types (again).

Following is an algorithm for testing structural type equivalence which handles recursive definitions properly. It does a parallel depth-first traversal of the two given types and uses a stack to hold pairs of **access** types it has seen along the way down.

```
                — The "assumption" environment
                SeenAccessTypes : STACK of
                                        record
                                                T1, T2 : TypeRef;
                                        end record := The_Empty_Stack;

        function Struct_Equiv(T1, T2: in TypeRef) return Boolean is
            result : Boolean;
        begin
            while T1.Form = SubTypes loop      — we always compare base types
                T1 := T1.BaseType;
            end loop;
            while T2.Form = SubTypes loop
                T2 := T2.BaseType;
            end loop;
            if (T1.Form /= T2.Form) then      — no chance to be equivalent
                return False;
            end if;

            case T1.Form is
                when Integer | FloatType | StringType | EnumType =>
                    return True;              — since T1.Form = T2.Form
                when ArrayType =>
                    return Struct_Equiv_Index_List(T1.IndexTypes, T2.IndexTypes) and
                            Struct_Equiv(T1.ElementType, T2.ElementType);
                when RecordType =>
                    return Struct_Equiv_Field_List(T1.FieldList, T2.FieldList) and
                        Struct_Equiv_Variant_List(T1.VariantList, T2.variatList);
                when IncompleteType | PrivateType =>
                    return T1 = T2;           — must be "identical" to be equivalent
                when AccessType =>
                    if T1 = T2 or
                        (T1, T2) is on SeenAccessTypes or
                        (T2, T1) is on SeenAccessTypes then
                            return True;
                    end if;
                    Push (T1, T2) onto SeenAccessTypes;
                    result := Struct_Equiv(T1.ReferencedType, T2.ReferencedType);
                    Pop(SeenAccessTypes);
                    return result;
                when others =>
                    return False;
            end case;
        end Struct_Equiv;
```

Struct_Equiv_Index_List, Struct_Equiv_Field_List, and Struct_Equiv_Variant_List just call Struct_Equiv recursively for each pair of members on the corresponding lists (and perhaps do some additional checking such as verifying that field names are the same). They return false if the result of checking any pair is false, otherwise they return true.

3.   Construct the Attributes records that correspond to each of the following declarations:

```
            A : constant Integer := 10;
            B : Integer;
            C : Integer := B+10;
```

Ans: (See Figure 10.17 for the type definitions of Attributes and Address)

```
        A = Attributes'(Class => Const,
                        Id => the IdEntry for A,
                        IdType => the TypeDescriptor of Integer,
                        Value => 10);

        B = Attributes'(Class => Variable,
                        Id => the IdEntry for B,
                        IdType => the TypeDescriptor of Integer,
                        VarAddress => Address'(VarLevel => Current_Nesting_Level,
                                               VarOffset => Current_AR_Offset,
                                               Indirect => False,
                                               Readonly => False))

        C = Attributes'(Class => Variable,
                        Id => the IdEntry for C,
                        IdType => the TypeDescriptor of Integer,
                        VarAddress => Address'(...))  — similar to that of B
```

Note that if C were defined to be a **constant**, its Attributes record would still be of class Variable, but the value of VarAddress.Readonly would be True.

5. Describe how TypeDescriptor and the action routines for handling incomplete types (in Section 10.3.6) would have to be changed to handle multiple dependent types for an incomplete type declaration.

Ans: To handle multiple dependent types for an incomplete type declaration, the DependentType field of the TypeDescriptor for an incomplete type would have to be a *list* of TypeRef instead of a single TypeRef. That is, in the definition of TypeDescriptor, we'd make the change:

```
    when IncompleteType => DependentTypes : TypeList;
```

Where

```
    type TypeList = access TypeListNode;
    type TypeListNode = record
                            ThisType : TypeRef;
                            NextNode : TypeList;
                        end record;
```

The semantic routine AccessType (p.365, Section 10.3.6) would be changed as:

```
AccessType(<subtype>) => <type definition>
    ...
    — T is the type descriptor for the defining access type
    If T.ReferencedType.Form = IncompleteType then
        Create a new TypeListNode, N, with value
        TypeListNode'(ThisType => T,
                        NextNode => T.ReferencedType.DependentTypes);
        T.ReferencedType.DependentTypes := N;
    end if;
    ...
```

The semantic routine TypeDecl (p.331, Section 10.2.2) would also need some extensions:

```
TypeDecl(<id>, <type definition>)
    If <id>.IdRecord.Id is already in the symbol table and its attribute
        record says it's an incomplete type declaration
    then
        Let I be the associated (incomplete) type descriptor.
        Let T be the type descriptor created by <type definition>
        Follow I.DependentTypes and update each of the type descriptor, D, on the
        list (which should be a descriptor for access types) by assigning T to
        D.ReferencedType.
        Update <id>'s attribute record, R, by setting R.IdType to T.
    else
        — new definition, enter the type declaration into the symbol table
    ...
    end if
```

6. Describe the data structure and action routine extensions necessary to check that all private types declared in the visible part of a package are completed within the corresponding private part.

Ans: First we add one field PrivateTypes, which is used to link all private type definitions in a package, to the attribute records of packages:

```
when PackageName => Scope : SymbolTablePackage.SymbolTable;
                    PrivateTypes : TypeList;
                    — used to link all private types in a package
```

The type TypeList is defined in exercise 5.

In the semantic routine PrivateTypeDecl (p.369, Section 10.3.7), if A is the newly created attribute record for the give private type declaration, we would add A.IdType to the list CurrentPackage.PrivateTypes.

Now the routine EndPackage (p.367, Section 10.3.7) must be extended to check if every type descriptor T, on the list CurrentPackage.PrivateTypes, has its TheType field filled in with some type definition (i.e. T.TheType /= **null**). Otherwise some private types are not completed.

Alternatively, we could add a new action routine after <private part> solely for this checking in order to detect and report errors earlier.

7.   Explain the error handling that must be done in the semantic routines that handle the following type declaration if T is undefined:

type A **is array** (1..10) **of array** (1..10) **of** T;

Ans: As soon as the semantic routine TypeReference (p.332, Section 10.2.2) finds that T is undefined, it should:

(1)   Generate an error message saying that T is undefined,

(2)   Enter T into the symbol table of current scope with attributes

                Attributes'(Class => TypeName,
                            Id => IdEntry for T,
                            IdType => TypeDescriptor'(Form => ErrorType,
                                                       Size => 0)),

(3)   Push an ErrorRecord onto the semantic stack.

The semantic routines for handling array type definitions will find that the component type is an ErrorRecord so they just propagate the error by returning another ErrorRecord. Finally when the error reaches routine TypeDecl, it would then create an ErrorType descriptor as the definition for type name A.

8.   Describe the data structure changes and the additional predefined identifiers that are necessary to add Boolean to the list of predefined types described in Section 10.2.2.

Ans: Since Boolean is just an enumeration type of two constants, False and True, we can simply use the definition of TypeDescriptor that includes a variant for enumeration types (see Section 10.3.2, and also Figure 10.17) to construct a type descriptor for Boolean type. First we enter the identifier Boolean into the symbol table (of global scope) with following attribute record:

            Attributes'(Class => TypeName,
                        Id => the IdEntry for Boolean,
                        IdType => TypeDescriptor'(Form => EnumType,
                                                   Size => IntegerSize,
                                                   FirstConst => the False attribute record))

The identifiers False and True are then created as predefined enumeration constants with following attributes:

— the False attribute record
Attribute'(Class => EnumConst,
            EnumValue => 0,
            NextConst => the True attribute record)

— the True attribute record
Attribute'(Class => EnumConst,
            EnumValue => 1,
            NextConst => **null**)

10.   Give examples of type definitions that illustrate the use of the four variants of the ConstraintDescriptor record defined in Figure 10.17.

Ans:

(a)   Dynamic range

   subtype T **is** Integer **range** N .. M;   — where N, M are variables

(b)   Static Range

   subtype T **is** Integer **range** 0 .. 10;

(c)   Unconstrained Index

   array (Integer **range** <>) **of** Integer;

(d)   Array Ranges

   array (1 .. 10) **of** Integer;

16.   Packages have two features that require special handling by the symbol table implementation: (a) A subset of the identifiers declared in the package are exported and (b) the package scope, perhaps containing some hidden identifiers, must be saved during the interval between the compilation times of the specification part and the package body. In light of these requirements, how would you design a symbol table implementation to accommodate packages?

Ans: See Section 8.4.2, Export Rules, and Section 8.4.3, Import Rules, (pp. 269-77) for some ideas.

17.   The implementation of private types presented in Section 10.3.7 is somewhat simplified by the fact that packages may not be nested in Ada/CS. What simplification does this restriction allow? Describe how the presented technique might be extended to support nested packages.

Ans: In Ada/CS, packages may not be nested. This restriction simplifies checking where the details of the representation of a private type can be accessed: we simply check if CurrentPackage is the same as the ContainingPackage of the private type descriptor. If we allow nested packages, we must use techniques similar to how **with** statements are handled (such as a dedicated scope stack for opening packages) in order to check if the representation of a private type is visible at certain point. For example, when a type T is found to be private, we must check if its ContainingPackage is on current package stack, if so, that means CurrentPackage is the same package, or lies *within* the package, where T is defined, and T's representation is visible at that point.

6.9. Chapter 11 Solutions

2. Write code to implement the NewName action routine outlined in Section 11.2.1, showing how a DataObject record is created to represent an identifier using information in the symbol table.

Ans:

```
NewName(<id>) => <simple name>

        SymbolTableRecord : IdEntryType;
        Object : DataObjectType;

        SymbolTableRecord <— SearchSymbolTable(<id>);
        if SymbolTableRecord = None then
          <simple name> <— an Error Record
        else
          with Object, SymbolTableRecord.Attributes do
          begin
            ObjectType <— IdType;
            Form <— Class;
            case Form is
                when ObjectValue => Value <— IdValue;
                when ObjectAddr => Addr <— VarAddress;
            end case;
          end;
          <simple name> <— Object;
        end if;
```

3.   Outline the routines SelectUnaryOperator and SelectBinaryOperator used by the semantic action routines in Section 11.2.2.

Ans:

```
SelectBinaryOperator(Operand1Record, OpRecord, Operand2Record)
                                          => TupleOp, ResultType
        if (OpRecord = Error record) or
           (Operand1Record = Error record) or
           (Operand2Record = Error record) then
           TupleOp ← None
        elsif TypeCompatible(OpRecord.Op, Operand1Record.ObjectType,
                              Operand2Record.ObjectType) then
              — This function determines whether the types of the
                operands conform to any of the definitions of Op.
           TupleOp ← SelectDefinition(Oprecord.Op,
                        OperandRecord1.ObjectType,
                        OperandRecord2.ObjectType);
              — This function selects a definition that is compatible
                with the operand types.
           if CoercionRequired(TupleOp, Operand1Record.ObjectType) or
              CoercionRequired(TupleOp, Operand2Record.ObjectType) then
              Generate tuples required for coercion of the operands;
              Modify the OperandRecords to reflect the change of type;
           end if;
           ResultType ← ResultTypeOf(TupleOp)
        else TupleOp ← None
        end if;
```

5.   What tuples would be generated for each of the following Ada/CS statements given these declarations?

```
I, J, K : Integer;
X, Y, Z : Float;
```

a.   I := −(J + 5);

Ans:

(1) (ADDI, J, 5, t1)

(2) (UMINUS, t1, t2)

(3) (ASSIGN, t2, 1, I)

b.   J := I * 2 − J * 3 + K / 4;

Ans:

      (1) (MULTI, I, 2, t1)
      (2) (MULTI, J, 3, t2)
      (3) (SUBI, t1, t2, t3)
      (4) (DIVI, K, 4, t4)
      (5) (ADDI, t3, t4, t5)
      (6) (ASSIGN, t5, 1, J)

c.   X := Y * 3.5 + Z / Float(I);

Ans:

      (1) (MULTF, Y, 3.5, t1)
      (2) (FLOAT, I, t2)
      (3) (DIVF, Z, t2, t3)
      (4) (ADDF, t1, t3, t4)
      (5) (ASSIGN, t4, 1, X)

6.   Show the offsets assigned to the fields in the following record declaration:

```
R : record
        X : Float;
        I, J : Integer;
        A : array (1..10, 5..9) of Float;
        R : record
                S : String;
                L : Integer;
            end record;
        S, T : String;
    end record;
```

Ans:

Declaration	Field Offsets
R : **record**	
X : Float;	0
I,	1
J : Integer;	2
A : **array** (1..10, 5..9) **of** Float;	3
R : **record**	53
S : String;	0
L : Integer;	1
end record;	
S,	55
T : String;	56
end record;	

7.   Give the sequence of action routine calls generated during the processing of each of the statements in Figure 11.5(b) and for each action routine indicate which, if any, of the tuples it produced.

Ans:

Action Routines	Tuples generated
NewName	
NewName	
ProcessIndex	(SUBI, Addr(A1), 2, t1)
	(RANGETEST, 1, 10, I)
	(MULTI, I, 2, t2)
	(ADDI, t1, t2, t3)
NewName	
Assign	(ASSIGN, ARecord, 2, @t3)
NewName	
FieldName	
NewName	
Assign	(ASSIGN, I, 1, @(Addr(ARecord)+1)))
NewName	
NewName	
ProcessIndex	(SUBI, Addr(A2), 20, t4)
	(RANGETEST, 4, 6, I)
	(MULTI, I, 5, t5)
	(ADDI, t4, t5, t6)
NewName	
ProcessIndex	(SUBI, t6, 8, t7)
	(RANGETEST, 8,12, J)
	(ADDI, t7, J, t8)
NewName	
NewName	
ProcessIndex	(SUBI, Addr(A1), 2, t9)
	(RANGETEST, 1,10, J)
	(MULTI, J, 2, t10)
	(ADDI, t9, t10, t11)
FieldName	(ADDI, t11, 1, t12)
Assign	(ASSIGN, @t12, 1, @t8)

8.   Using the declarations from Figure 11.5(a), what tuples would be generated for the following statements?

a.   A1(5) := A1(I+J);

Ans:

(1) (SUBI, Addr(A1), 2, t1)

(2) (ADDI, t1, 10, t2)   — 10 = 5 * element size
                                — t2 contains address of A1(5)

(3) (ADDI, I, J, t4)

(4) (SUBI, Addr(A1), 2, t3)

(5) (RANGETEST, 1, 10, t4)

(6) (MULTI, t4, 2, t5)

(7) (ADDI, t3, t5, t6)   — t6 contains address of A1(I+J)

(8) (ASSIGN, @t6, 2, @t2)

b.   A2(ARecord.X, ARecord.Y) := J;

Ans:

(1) (SUBI, Addr(A2), 20, t1)

(2) (RANGETEST, 4, 6, @(Addr(ARecord)))

(3) (MULTI, @(Addr(ARecord)), 5, t2)   — 5 = element size of

— second component of A2

(4) (ADDI, t1, t2, t3)

(5) (SUBI, t3, 8, t4)

(6) (RANGETEST, 8, 12, @(Addr(ARecord)+1))

(7) (ADDI, t4, @(Addr(ARecord)+1), t5)

(8) (ASSIGN, J, 1, @t5)

c.   A1(A1(I).Y).X := J * 3;

Ans:

(1) (SUBI, Addr(A1), 2, t1)

(2) (RANGETEST, 1, 10, I)

(3) (MULTI, I, 2, t2)   — 2 = element size of A1

(4) (ADDI, t1, t2, t3)   — t3 contains the address of A1(I)

(5) (ADDI, t3, 1, t4)   — t4 contains the address of A1(I).Y

(6) (SUBI, Addr(A1), 2, t5)

(7) (RANGETEST, 1, 10, @t4)

(8) (MULTI, @t4, 2, t6)

(9) (ADDI, t5, t6, t7)

— Offset for X is 0. Addition not

— necessary.

(10) (MULTI, J, 3, t8)

(11) (ASSIGN, t8, 1, @t7)

d.   A2(I,9) := A2(5,J);

Ans:

(1) (SUBI, Addr(A2), 20, t1)
(2) (RANGETEST, 4, 6, I)
(3) (MULTI, I, 5, t2)
(4) (ADDI, t1, t2, t3)
(5) (SUBI, t3, 8, t4)
(6) (ADDI, t4, 9, t5)
(7) (SUBI, Addr(A2), 20, t6)
(8) (ADDI, t6, 25, t7)   — 25 = 5 * Element Size
(9) (SUBI, t7, 8, t8)
(10) (RANGETEST, 8, 12, J)
(11) (ADDI, t8, J, t9)
(12) (ASSIGN, @t9, 1, @t5)

9.   Outline the run-time routines required to implement string comparison, substring access and catenation assuming the dynamic string implementation discussed in Section 11.2.4.

Ans: The routines below assume that each string variable is represented by a pointer to the dynamically created string object as well as the current size of the string. Whether the size is stored at the string object or at the string variable location is irrelevant to these routines.

```
StringEqual(<string₁>, <string₂>) => <result>
      Equal : boolean;

      If <string₁>.size /= <string₂>.size then
        Equal ← false
      else
        Equal ← true;
        for i In 0 .. <string₁>.size–1 loop
          If <string₁> object(i) /=
            <string₂> object(i) then
              Equal ← false;
              exit;
          end if;
        end loop;
      end if;
      <result> ← Equal;
```

The routines for other string comparisons are similar.

```
SubString(<string>, start, length) => <result>
        if (start+length−1) > <string>.size then
            <result> ← null string
        else
            Allocate memory for a string object of size length;
            <result>.addr ← Start address of allocated memory;
            <result>.size ← length;
            for i in 0 .. length−1 loop
                <result> object(i) ← <string> object(start+i)
            end loop;
        end if;


StringCatenate(<string₁>, <string₂>) => <result>
```

$$StringCatenate(<string_1>, <string_2>) => <result>$$

$$<result>.size \leftarrow <string_1>.size + <string_2>.size;$$

```
        Allocate memory for a string object of size <result>.size;
        <result>.addr ← starting address of the allocated memory;
        Copy <string₁> object into <result> object starting
                from <result>.addr;
        Copy <string₂> object into <result> object starting
                from <result>.addr + <string₁>.size;
```

11. If arrays are being implemented using run-time type descriptors like those in Figure 11.11

     a.   Show the type descriptors that would be generated for

            type T **is array** (1..M) **of array** (2..N) **of** Float;

Ans:

L=1	U=?	Size=?	descriptor for Type&2
L=2	U=?	Size=?	descriptor for Type&1

     b.   If A and B are declared to be of type T within the the same procedure in which T is declared, show an activation record for that procedure illustrating all of the data objects related to A, B and T.

Ans:

Data area for A
. . .
Data area for B
. . .
. . .
Data area address for B
Data area address for A
descriptor for Type&2
descriptor for Type&1
. . .

c.   Show how the type descriptors look after the procedure is entered with M = 5 and N = 8.

Ans:

L=1	U=5	Size=35	descriptor for Type&2
L=2	U=8	Size=7	descriptor for Type&1

d.   What tuples would be generated for

   A(I,J) := B(1,I) + B(J,2);

Ans:

        (1) (RANGETEST, 1, Type&2(Upper), I)
        (2) (SUBI, I, 1, t1)
        (3) (MULTI, t1, Type&2(Size), t2)
        (4) (ADDI, Addr(A), t2, t3)
        (5) (RANGETEST, 2, Type&1(Upper), J)
        (6) (SUBI, J, 2, t4)
        (7) (MULTI, t4, Type&1(Size), t5)
        (8) (ADDI, t3, t5, t6)
        (9) (RANGETEST, 1, Type&2(Upper), 1)
        (10) (RANGETEST, 2, Type&1(Upper), I)
        (11) (SUBI, I, 2, t7)
        (12) (MULTI, t7, Type&1(Size), t8)
        (13) (ADDI, Addr(B), t8, t9)
        (14) (RANGETEST, 1, Type&2(Upper), J)
        (15) (SUBI, J, 1, t10)
        (16) (MULTI, t10, Type&2(Size), t11)
        (17) (ADDI, Addr(B), t11, t12)
        (18) (RANGETEST, 2, Type&1(Upper), 2)
        (19) (ADDI, @t9,@t12, t13)
        (20) (ASSIGN, t13, 1, @t6)

13. Show the tuples generated for the following expression using the type descriptors defined in Figure 11.15:

$$X(I).C+X(I).E(J)$$

Ans:

```
(1)  (RANGETEST, T4(Lower), T4(Upper), I)
(2)  (SUBI, I, T4(Lower), t1)
(3)  (ADDI, Addr(X), t1, t2)
(4)  (ADDI, t2, 1, t3)
(5)  (RANGETEST, T4(Lower), T4(Upper), I)
(6)  (SUBI, I, T4(Lower), t4)
(7)  (ADDI, Addr(X), t4, t5)
(8)  (ADDI, t5, T3(E), t6)
(9)  (RANGETEST, T2(Lower), T2(Upper), J)
(10) (SUBI, J, T2(Lower), t7)
(11) (ADDI, t6, t7, t8)
(12) (ADDI, @t3, @t8, t9)                   — t9 holds the result
```

14. Given the following declarations and assuming that the offset of I is 5:

```
I : Integer;
R : record
      F1 : Integer;
      case T1 : Integer range 1..2 is
          when 1 => F2 : Integer;
          when 2 => case T2 : Integer range 3..4 is
                       when 3 => F3 : Integer;
                       when 4 => F4 : Integer;
                                 F5 : Integer;
                    end case;
      end case;
   end record;
```

What tuples, including variant checks, would be generated for the following statements? Assume that the offsets are relative to the value in a base register B.

a.   I := R.F1;

Ans: (1) (ASSIGN, (B,6), 1, (B,5))

b.   R.F1 := R.F2;

Ans:

(1) (RANGETEST, 1, 1, (B,7))
(2) (ASSIGN, (B,8), 1, (B,6))

c.   R.F4 := I + R.F5;

Ans:

      (1) (RANGETEST, 2, 2, (B,7))

      (2) (RANGETEST, 4, 4, (B,8))

      (3) (RANGETEST, 2, 2, (B,7))

      (4) (RANGETEST, 4, 4, (B,8))

      (5) (ADDI, (B,5), (B,10), t1)

      (6) (ASSIGN, t1, 1, (B,9))

15.   The checking technique described in Section 11.3.4 for verifying the validity of pointers to dynamic objects can be defeated by a Pascal program that declares a variant record that overlays pointers to two different types of objects with different sizes. For example,

```
R : record
      case T1 :  Boolean of
          True:   (P1 : ↑ array [1..10] Integer;);
          False:  (P2 : ↑ array [1..100] Integer;);
    end;
```

Since the tag field (T1) can be changed without altering the rest of the information in the record, a dangerous situation exists following a call to new(P1) and an assignment of False to T1. A reference to R.P2↑[50] will pass a variant check, a pointer validity check and a subscript check, but it will refer to a place in the heap not allocated by the call to new that created the pointer. Explain how the pointer checking mechanism could be extended to signal an error in such cases.

Ans: The number of bits in the lock and key can be extended to include type information. If the number of possible types is not too large, the bits representing the type can be appended to the original lock and key bits. Otherwise, the type code can be hashed to a smaller range.

The compiler translates the call new(P1) into a system allocation routine that requires two parameters — the access object and an optional type code. The allocation routine creates the lock as before and adds on the type code bits to it. The key is returned as before. At every reference, the compiler generates code to compute the new key using the current type code and the key stored in the access object. The new key is then used for pointer validity check as before.

16.   If the operator + has the following definitions associated with it

      ((float, float) —> float)

      ((integer, integer) —> integer)

      ((integer, integer) —> float)

If I and J are integers and F is a float, explain how the BuildTree routine in Figure 11.17 would be used to interpret the expression I+J+F.

Ans: The first invocation of BuildTree analyzes the expression I+J. The ArgList is:

((integer), (integer))

When BuildTree compares the definitions associated with + to ArgList, both the second and the third definitions match and BuildTree returns a list of two trees:

(((integer),(integer) $\longrightarrow$ (integer)), ((integer),(integer) $\longrightarrow$ (float)))

For the second invocation of BuildTree, the ArgList is:

((((integer),(integer) $\longrightarrow$ (integer)), ((integer),(integer) $\longrightarrow$ (float))), (float))

When BuildTree compares the definitions associated with + to this ArgList, only the arguments of the first definition match using the second subtree in the first TreeList and the only tree in the second TreeList. BuildTree then returns the single tree,

((((integer),(integer) $\longrightarrow$ (float)), (float)) $\longrightarrow$ (float))

as the interpretation of the given expression.

6.10. Chapter 12 Solutions

1. Trace the sequence of semantic routine calls that occur during the compilation of the following program fragments. Show the tuples that are generated, with an indication of which routine generates each tuple. Assume that I, J, and K are all Integer variables.

    a. **If** I > J **then**
          K := I;
        elsif J > I **then**
          K := J;
        else
          K := 0;
        end If;

    Ans: Note: Calls to routines NewName and ProcessOp have been ignored in the solutions below:

Semantic Routines	Tuples generated
StartIf	
EvalBinary	(GT, I, J, t1)
IfTest	(JUMP0, t1, L2)
Assign	(ASSIGN, I, 1, K)
GenJump	(JUMP, L1)
GenElseLabel	(LABEL, L2)
EvalBinary	(GT, J, I, t2)
IfTest	(JUMP0, t2, L3)
Assign	(ASSIGN, J, 1, K)
GenJump	(JUMP, L1)
GenElseLabel	(LABEL, L3)
Assign	(ASSIGN, K, 1, 0)
GenOutLabel	(LABEL, L1)

    b. **If** I > J **then**
          K := I;
        elsif J >= I **then**
          K := J;
        end If;

    Ans: Similar to above solution.

2. Trace the sequence of semantic routine calls that occur during the compilation of the following program fragment. Show the tuples that are generated, with an indication of which routine generates each tuple. Assume that I, J, Limit and Sum are Integer variables and A is a two-dimensional array of Integer.

```
                    Sum : = 0;
                    I := 0;
         OuterLoop: loop
                       I := I + 1;
                       exit when I > Limit;
                       J := 1;
                       while J <= Limit loop
                         exit OuterLoop when A(I,J) = 0;
                         Sum := Sum + A(I,J);
                         J := J + 1;
                       end loop;
                    end loop;
```

Ans: Note: Calls to routines NewName and ProcessOp have been ignored in the solution below:

Semantic Routines	Tuples generated
Assign	(ASSIGN, Sum, 1, 0)
Assign	(ASSIGN, I, 1, 0)
GenLoopLabel	(LABEL, L1)
EvalBinary	(ADDI, I, 1, t1)
Assign	(ASSIGN, I, 1, t1)
NullName	
EvalBinary	(GT, I, Limit, t2)
ExitCond	(JUMP1, t2, L2)
Assign	(ASSIGN, 1, 1, J)
StartWhile	(LABEL, L3)
EvalBinary	(LE, J, Limit, t3)
WhileTest	(JUMP0, t3, L4)
ProcessName	
StartIndex	({RANGETEST for I})
Index	({RANGETEST for J})
FinishIndex	({Tuples to compute address of A(I,J) in t4})
EvalBinary	(EQ, @(t4), 0, t5)
ExitCond	(JUMP1, t5, L2)
StartIndex	({RANGETEST for I})
Index	({RANGETEST for J})
FinishIndex	({Tuples to compute address of A(I,J) in t6})
EvalBinary	(ADDI, Sum, @(t6), t7)
Assign	(ASSIGN, t7, 1, Sum)
EvalBinary	(ADDI, J, 1, t8)
Assign	(ASSIGN, t8, 1, J)
FinishWhile	(JUMP, L3)
	(LABEL, L4)
LoopBack	(JUMP, L1)
	(LABEL, L2)

3. Trace the sequence of semantic routine calls that occur during the compilation of the following program fragment. Show the tuples that are generated, with an indication of which routine generates each tuple. Assume that I and Limit are Integer variables and B is a one-dimensional array of Integer.

```
      Sum := 0;
      for I in 1..Limit loop
         Sum := Sum + B(I);
      end loop;
```

Ans: Note: Calls to routines NewName and ProcessOp have been ignored in the solution below:

Semantic Routines	Tuples generated
Assign	(ASSIGN, 0, 1, Sum)
EnterForId	
InitLoop	(GT, 1, Limit, t2)
	(JUMP1, t2, L1)
	(ASSIGN, 1, 1, t1)
	(ASSIGN, Limit, 1, t3)
	(LABEL, L2)
StartIndex	({RANGETEST for I})
FinishIndex	({Tuples to compute address of B(I) in t4})
EvalBinary	(ADDI, Sum, @(t4), t5)
Assign	(ASSIGN, t5, 1, Sum)
FinishLoop	(EQ, t1, t3, t6)
	(JUMP1, t6, L1)
	(ADDI, t1, 1, t1)
	(JUMP, L2)
	(LABEL, L1)

4.   Write a **case** statement with at least six labeled alternatives plus an **others** alternative. The labels should include ranges as well as single values. Trace the sequence of semantic routine calls that would occur during the compilation of your **case** statement. Show the tuples that are generated by all action routines other than FinishCase and diagram the data structures created to describe the labels of the alternatives.

Ans:

```
      case Tag is
         when 0 => I := 1;
         when 1 => I := 0;
         when 5 .. 9 => I := 2;
         when 10  => I := 3;
         when 11 .. 98 => I := 4;
         when 99 | 100 => I := 99;
         when others => I := 100;
      end case;
```

Semantic Routines	Tuples generated
StartCase	(LT, Tag, MinChoice?, t1)
	(JUMP1, t1, L1)
	(GT, Tag, MaxChoice?, t2)
	(JUMP1, t2, L1)
	(LABEL, L2)
	(JUMPX, Tag, TableLabel?-MinChoice?)
AppendValOrSubType	(LABEL, L4)
Assign	(ASSIGN, 1, 1, I)
FinishChoice	(JUMP, L3)
AppendValOrSubType	(LABEL, L5)
Assign	(ASSIGN, 0, 1, I)
FinishChoice	(JUMP, L3)
AppendRange	(LABEL, L6)
Assign	(ASSIGN, 2, 1, I)
FinishChoice	(JUMP, L3)
AppendValOrSubType	(LABEL, L7)
Assign	(ASSIGN, 3, 1, I)
FinishChoice	(JUMP, L3)
AppendRange	(LABEL, L8)
Assign	(ASSIGN, 4, 1, I)
FinishChoice	(JUMP, L3)
AppendValOrSubType	(LABEL, L9)
AppendValOrSubType	(LABEL, L10)
Assign	(ASSIGN, 99, 1, I)
FinishChoice	(JUMP, L3)
StartOthers	(LABEL, L1)
Assign	(ASSIGN, 100, 1, I)
FinishChoice	(JUMP, L3)
FinishCase	

ChoiceList →	LowerBnd	UpperBnd	StartLabel
	0	0	L4
	1	1	L5
	5	9	L6
	10	10	L7
	11	98	L8
	99	99	L9
	100	100	L10

5. Show the tuples that would be generated by FinishCase for your **case** statement from Exercise 4 using the jump table approach.

Ans: The tuples generated by StartCase would be backpatched as follows:

(LT, Tag, 0, t1)
(GT, Tag, 100, t2)
(JUMPX, Tag, L11-0)

The tuples generated by FinishCase are:

```
(LABEL, L11)
(JUMP, L4)
(JUMP, L5)
(JUMP, L1)
    ... {Three more jumps to L1}
(JUMP, L6)
    ... {Four more jumps to L6}
(JUMP, L7)
(JUMP, L8)
    ... {87 more jumps to L8}
(JUMP, L9)
(JUMP, L10)
(LABEL, L3)
```

7.   Rewrite the semantic routine outlines and semantic record declarations for compiling basic **loop**s and **while loop**s to use backpatching rather than symbolic labels to handle jump address resolution. (Hint: See the discussion of backpatching at the end of Section 12.1.)

Ans: Backpatching is not necessary for a basic loop statement. However, the tuple number can be used instead of the symbolic label. The semantic record would then be:

```
type LabelType is
  record
    Label : TupleNumberType;
  end record;
```

The two semantic routines are modified as follows:

```
GenLoopLabel () => loop
  L <— Next Tuple number;
  loop <— LabelType'(Label => L)

LoopBack (loop)
  Generate(JUMP, loop.LabelRecord.Label)
```

For the **while** statement, a single backpatch is necessary for the Out label. The semantic record for the **while** loop must store the start tuple number and the tuple number of the jump to Out label. The semantic record will be as follows:

```
type WhileStmtType is
  record
    StartTuple, JumpOutTuple : TupleNumberType;
  end record;
```

The semantic routines are modified as follows:

```
StartWhile () => while
  L <— Next Tuple number;
  while <— WhileStmtType'(StartTuple => L,
                         JumpOutTuple => 0)
```

```
WhileTest (while, <b expr>) => while
  Check that <b expr>.DataObjectRecord.ObjectType = Boolean
  while.WhileStmtRecord.JumpOutTuple <— Next Tuple number;
  Generate(JUMP0, <b expr>.DataObjectRecord, 0);
  while <— the updated WhileStmt record


FinishWhile (while)
  Generate(JUMP, while.WhileStmtRecord.StartTuple);
  L <— Next Tuple number;
  BackPatch(while.WhileStmtRecord.JumpOutTuple, L)
```

8. Rewrite the semantic routine outlines and semantic record declarations for compiling **if** statements to use backpatching rather than symbolic labels to handle jump address resolution.

Ans: The semantic record is:

```
type IfStmtType is
  record
    JumpOutTuples : TupleListType;
    LastElseJump : TupleNumberType;
  end record;
```

The semantic routines are modified as follows:

```
StartIf () => if
  if <— IfStmtType'(JumpOutTuples => Nil, LastElseJump => 0)


IfTest (if, <b expr>) => if
  Check that <b expr>.DataObjectRecord.ObjectType = Boolean
  L <— Next Tuple Number;
  if.IfStmtRecord.LastElseJump <— L;
  Generate(JUMP0, <b expr>.DataObjectRecord, 0);
  if <— the updated IfStmt record


GenJump (if) => if
  L <— Next Tuple number;
  Append L to if.IfStmtRecord.JumpOutTuples;
  Generate(JUMP, 0);
  if <— the updated IfStmt record


GenElseLabel (if)
  L <— Next Tuple number;
  BackPatch(if.IfStmtRecord.LastElseJump, L);


GenOutLabel (if)
  L <— Next Tuple number;
  for i in if.IfStmtRecord.JumpOutTuples loop
    BackPatch(i, L);
  end loop
```

10. Explain the processing done by a compiler for the labels and **goto**s in the following Ada program fragment, according to the technique summarized in Figure 12.6.

Ans:

```
          declare
            . . .
          begin
            <<L>>
              {New resolved entry:
                 Store <L, L1, Resolved> in symbol table;
                 Generate (LABEL, L1); }
            declare
              . . .
            begin
              . . .
                goto L;
                  { S <— SymboltableEntry("L");
                    New Unresolved Entry: — Since the entry in the table
                       — is for a declaration in an outer block, must wait
                       — and see if there is a declaration further ahead
                       — in the current block.
                    N <— NextTupleNumber;
                    Generate(JUMP, ?);
                    Store <L, <N>, Unresolved> in symbol table; }
                . . .
                goto M;
                  {New Unresolved Entry: — There is no entry for M
                            — in the symbol table.
                    N <— NextTupleNumber;
                    Generate(JUMP, ?);
                    Store <M, <N>, Unresolved> in symbol table; }
                . . .
                <<M>>
                  {Resolve:
                    Get the entry <M, <N>, Unresolved> from
                                 symbol table;
                    BackPatch(N, L2);
                    Generate(LABEL, L2);
                    Replace the entry for M in the symbol table with
                         <M, L2, Resolved> }
                . . .
            end;
              {Flush:
                    Entry for M is removed from symbol table;
                    Get entry for L from symbol table; — from current level
                    Since it is unresolved check for a resolved entry
                    in the next level;
                  Generate: — In this case there is a resolved entry for L
                            — in the next level;
                    BackPatch(N,L1) — N is the tuple number from the
                                 — unresolved entry for L }
              . . .
          end;
            {Flush:
              Entry for L is removed from symbol table }
```

11. Using the techniques of Section 12.6, illustrate the significant address ranges, the exception transfer vectors and range map for the following program. Explain how the **raise** statement within procedure Q is handled and how the occurrence of a Constraint_Error exception within Q is handled.

———————	**procedure** P **is**
	. . .
Range 1	Fault : **exception**;
———————	**procedure** Q **is**
	begin
	. . .
Range 2	**raise** Fault;
	. . .
———————	**exception**
Range 3	**when** Fault => · · · ;
———————	**end** Q;
	begin
Range 4	. . .
	Q;
	. . .
———————	**exception**
Range 5	**when** Constraint_Error => · · · ;
———————	**end** P;

Ans: The transfer vectors are:

	Transfer Vector		Default
TV1			PropagateException
TV2	Constraint_Error		PropagateException
TV3		Fault	PropagateException

The Range Map is:

range 1	TV2
range 2	TV3
range 3	TV2
range 4	TV2
range 5	TV1

The **raise** statement in procedure Q is in address range 2. A lookup in the range table indicates that TV3 is the appropriate transfer vector. TV3 contains an entry for the Fault exception and a jump is made to the local handler.

There is no entry for Constraint_Error exception in TV3. Hence as a default, the control is passed to the PropagateException routine. This routine executes the code required for terminating the activation of Q and raises the exception again at the point immediately after the call to Q. This point is in address range 4 and TV2 is the appropriate transfer vector. TV2 has an entry for the Constraint_Error exception and control is transferred to the handler defined in P.

12. Using the techniques of Section 12.6, illustrate the significant address ranges, the exception transfer vectors and range map for the following program. Explain how the **raise** statement within procedure R is handled when it is called from Q and when it is called from P.

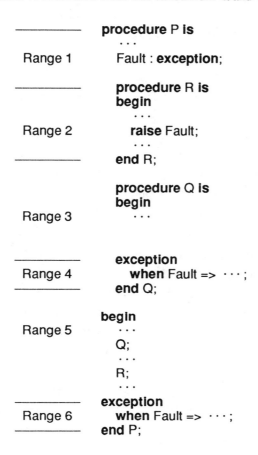

Ans: The transfer vectors are:

	Transfer Vector		Default
TV1			PropagateException
TV2	P.Fault		PropagateException
TV3	Q.Fault		PropagateException

The Range Map is:

range 1	TV2
range 2	TV1
range 3	TV3
range 4	TV2
range 5	TV2
range 6	TV1

The transfer vector appropriate for the **raise** statement in procedure R is TV1. TV1 contains just the default entry for PropagateException. When the Fault exception is raised in R, control is passed to the PropagateException routine. This routine performs the operations necessary for terminating the activation of R and raises the same exception after the point of call. If R was called from Q, the exception is raised again in the address range 3. The handler defined in Q will handle this exception according to TV3. If R was called from P, the exception is raised again in address range 5. In this case the handler defined in P will handle the exception according to TV2.

13. There are interesting interactions between exception handling features and an interactive debugger. Normally, such a debugger is invoked when a run-time error occurs. However, in a language with exception handling features, such errors are manifested as predefined exceptions. Thus the debugger is only invoked when no handler is supplied for an exception (predefined or defined in the program). Explain how the exception handling implementation techniques of Section 12.6 would have to be changed to interact with a debugger, given that the debugger should be given control with a view of the program state in which the unhandled exception was raised.

Ans: In the exception handling implementation, whenever an exception is raised for which there is no non-default handler, the debugger routine is invoked in the environment in which the exception originally was raised. In effect, the debugger acts as if it was called by a local handler for the exception. Thus while we are searching for the appropriate handler we must preserve the state (run-time stack) at which the exception was raised. When control returns from the debugger, execution resumes at the successor to the block, package or subprogram in which the exception was raised.

14. Using the technique presented in Section 12.7, do a trace like that in Figure 12.12 of the translation of

if A and B and then C or else not D then · · ·

Ans:

	Actions	Generated Code
(1)	StartOp (**and**)	
(2)	FinishOp (**and**) EvalBinary(A,**and**,B)	1 : (AND,A,B,t1)

(3)	StartOp (**and then**)
	ConvertToJumpCode(t1)
	  t1.TC = (2,3) t1.FC = (2,4)
	BackPatch t1.tc to 3
	  t1.TC = **null** t1.FC = (2,4)
		2 : (BR,t1,?,?)
		
		2 : (BR,t1,3,?)

(4)	FinishOp (**and then**)
	ConvertToJumpCode(C)
	  C.TC = (3,3) C.FC = (3,4)
	  Result2.TC = C.TC = (3,3)
	  Result2.FC = Merge(t1.FC,C.FC)=
	   ((2,4),(3,4))
		3 : (BR,C,?,?)

(5)	StartOp (**or else**)
	BackPatch Result2.FC to 4
	
	  Result2.TC = (3,3)
	  Result2.FC = **null**
		2 : (BR,t1,3,4)
		3 : (BR,C,?,4)

(6)	ProcessNot EvalUnary(**not**, D)	4 : (NOT, D, t1)

(7)	FinishOp (**or else**)
	ConvertToJumpCode(t1)
	  t1.TC = (5,3) t1.FC = (5,4)
	  Result3.TC = Merge(Result2.TC,t1.TC)=
	   ((3,3),(5,3))
	  Result3.FC = (5,4)
		5 : (BR,t1,?,?)

(8)	As **if** is processed BackPatch Result3.TC to ThenAdr BackPatch Result3.FC to ElseAdr	

15. Using the technique presented in Section 12.7.1, do a trace like that in Figure 12.14 of the translation of

> **if** A >= C **or else not** (C <> A **and then** B < 77) **then** A := B **end if**;

Ans:

	Actions	Generated Code	Semantic Stack (TChain, FChain, cond)
(a)	#Compare	1 : CMP A,C	(**null**,**null**,LT)
(b)	#FTF Append 2 to TC	2 : (B GE,?)	(2,**null**,LT)
	BackPatch FC to 3		(2,**null**,LT)
(c)	#Compare	3 : CMP C,A	(**null**,**null**,EQ)(2,**null**,LT)
(d)	#FTT Append 4 to FC	4 : B EQ,?	(**null**,4,EQ)(2,**null**,LT)
	BackPatch TC to 5		(**null**,4,EQ)(2,**null**,LT)
(e)	#Compare	5 : CMP B,77	(**null**,**null**,GE)(**null**,4,EQ)(2,**null**,LT)
(f)	#BoolOp		(**null**,4,GE)(2,**null**,LT)
(g)	#ProcessNot		(4,**null**,LT)(2,**null**,LT)
(h)	#BoolOp		(<4,2>,**null**,LT)
(i)	#FTT Append 6 to FC	6 : B LT,?	(<4,2>,6,LT)
	BackPatch TC to 7	2 : B GE,7 4 : B EQ,7	(**null**,6,LT)
(j)	#Assign	7 : ASSIGN B,A	
(k)	#PatchOutJumps BackPatch FC to 8	6 : B LT,8	(**null**,**null**,LT)

6.11. Chapter 13 Solutions

1. Explain how the SimpleProcStmt action routine of Section 13.1.2 and GenProcJump of Section 13.3 would have to be changed to handle functions as well as procedures.

Ans: The check for the ReturnType being **null** is removed from SimpleProcStmt. Both routines must update the semantic stack and possibly generate code to save the result returned by the function. If the function returns a scalar value in a temporary, a DataObjectRecord is created on the semantic stack holding the address of the temporary. The type of the result is obtained from the attributes of the symbol table record for the function. If the function returns the result in the memory location(s) above the activation record of the caller then code must be generated to either copy the result to a temporary or to extend the activation record size of the caller to include the result. A DataObjectRecord is placed on the semantic stack as before to hold the address and type of the result.

2. A call to a function with no parameters looks exactly like a reference to a variable. Determine which of the action routines presented in Chapter 11 would have to be modified to handle parameterless functions and describe the necessary modifications.

Ans: Parameterless functions can be handled by just modifying the NewName routine. When NewName looks up the name in the symbol table, it may get the attribute record for a subprogram. If it does then the NewName routine calls the SimpleProcStmt with the modifications described in Exercise 1.

7. Show the Attributes record, including parameter list for the following procedure declaration.

```
type A is array (1..20) of Integer;
procedure P (X : in Integer; InArray : in A; InOutArray : in out A);
begin
  for I in 1..20 loop
    InOutArray(I) := X * InArray(I);
  end loop;
end P;
```

Ans:

field	value	comment
Class	SubProgName	
Id	P	Pointer to the symbol table entry for P.
IdType	**null**	
NestingLevel	1	Assume that the declaration is at top level.
StartLabel	L1	L1 is the label of the first tuple of the body.
ActivationRecSize	ControlSize+1+1+20	Assuming a pointer to InArray is passed.
LocalDecls	NewSymbolTable	The symbol table will be empty.
Parameters	X	Pointer to attribute record for X.
ReturnType	**null**	
BodyDeclared	True	

field	value	comment
Class	ParamName	
Id	X	Pointer to symbol table entry for X.
IdType	Integer	TypeDescriptor for Integer.
ParamLevel	1	
ParamOffSet	0	
Mode	InMode	
NextParam	InArray	Pointer to attribute record for InArray.

field	value	comment
Class	ParamName	
Id	InArray	Pointer to symbol table entry for InArray.
IdType	A	TypeDescriptor for A.
ParamLevel	1	
ParamOffSet	1	
Mode	InMode	
NextParam	InOutArray	Pointer to attribute record for InOutArray.

field	value	comment
Class	ParamName	
Id	InOutArray	Pointer to symbol table entry for InOutArray.
IdType	A	TypeDescriptor for A.
ParamLevel	1	
ParamOffSet	2	
Mode	InOutMode	
NextParam	**null**	

8. Assuming that the array parameters are implemented by value or value-result, show the tuples generated for the procedure in Exercise 7. Use (level, offset) pairs to specify variables and parameters in the tuples, rather than symbolic names. Assume that P is declared at nesting level 2.

Ans: Assume that the caller copies the scalar parameters and the callee copies the non-scalar parameters.

```
(1) (JUMP, L1)                          — Execution of enclosing scope must jump
                                        — over this body.
(2) (LABEL, L2)                         — Start label for this procedure.
(3) (STARTSUBPROG, 3)
(4) (ASSIGN, @(3,1), 20, (3,1))         — (3,1) contained the address of the actual
                                        — parameter bound to InArray.
(5) (ASSIGN, @(3,21), 1, (3,22))        — Address of actual parameter bound to
                                        — InOutArray must be preserved.
(6) (ASSIGN, 1, 1, t1)                  — For loop variable is maintained in a temporary
(7) (LABEL, L3)
(8) (ADDRESS, (3,22), t2)               — t2 contains the address of InOutArray.
(9) (SUBI, t2, 1, t3)                   — t3 = Address(InOutArray)–Lower(A)
(10) (RANGETEST, 1, 20, t1)
(11) (ADDI, t3, t1, t4)                 — t4 = Address(InOutArray(I))
(12) (ADDRESS, (3,1), t5)               — t5 contains the address of InArray.
(13) (SUBI, t5, 1, t6)                  — t6 = Address(InArray)–Lower(A)
(14) (RANGETEST, 1, 20, t1)
(15) (ADDI, t6, t1, t7)                 — t7 contains the address of InArray(I).
(16) (MULTI, (3,0), @t7, t8)
(17) (ASSIGN, t8, 1, @t4)
(18) (EQ, t1, 20, t9)
(19) (JUMP1, t9, L4)
(20) (ADDI, t1, 1, t1)
(21) (JUMP, L3)
(22) (LABEL, L4)
(23) (ASSIGN, (3,22), 20, @(3,21))      — Copy InOutArray back.
(24) (ENDSUBPROG, 42+ControlSize)       — Activation record size = 1+20+1+20+ControlSize
(25) (LABEL, L1)
```

10.   Given the following declarations at the same level as P in Exercise 7,

A1, A2 : A;
J, K: Integer;

and that the offset of A1 is 5, show the tuples that would be generated for the call

P(J*K, A1, A2);

for each of the parameter implementations assumed in Exercises 8 and 9.

Ans: (1) Array parameters passed by value and value result:

Assume that actual copying of the value and result is done by the procedure.

```
(1) (STARTCALL, t1, 42+ControlSize)
(2) (MULTI, (2,45), (2,46), t2)
(3) (COPYIN, t2, 0, t1)                 — Copy value of J*K into X
(4) (COPYIN, (2,5), 1, t1)              — Copy the address of A1 into the first location
                                        — of InArray.
(5) (COPYINOUT, (2,25), 21, t1)         — Copy the address of A2 into the copy-back
                                        — address area of InOutArray.
(6) (PROCJUMP, L2, t1)
```

(2) Array parameters passed by reference:

```
(1) (STARTCALL, t1, 3+ControlSize)
(2) (MULTI, (2,45), (2,46), t2)
(3) (COPYIN, t2, 0, t1)          — Copy value of J*K into X
(4) (COPYIN, (2,5), 1, t1)       — Copy the address of A1 into InArray.
(5) (COPYINOUT, (2,25), 2, t1)   — Copy the address of A2 into InOutArray.
(6) (PROCJUMP, L2, t1)
```

11.   The subprogram call and return steps listed at the beginning of Section 13.4.2 assumed that it was the responsibility of the called subprogram to save all registers. Rewrite these call and return sequences for each of the other register save alternatives discussed in Section 13.4.1.

Ans: (1) Callee saves caller's registers:

Before the procedure is called, the caller pushes a bit/byte-vector onto the control part of the activation record. No space is allocated for register-save.

The callee, after being called, uses the bit/byte-vector to save the registers above the fixed-size part of the activation record using the local StackTop.

The callee, before exit, uses the bit/byte-vector to restore the saved registers.

(2) Caller saves caller's registers:

The caller, before the procedure is called, saves the registers being used by extending its own activation record and incrementing its local StackTop before it performs the other steps in the sequence. No space is allocated for saving registers in the callee's activation record.

The caller, after the called procedure returns, restores the registers from the top of its stack and resets the local StackTop. It may have to copy values returned by a function above the register-save area.

(3) Callee saves callee's registers:

The callee, after being called, executes code to save the registers in its activation record. This code may be at the end of the procedure and wired in to execute before the procedure body is executed or may be at the beginning using a bit/byte-vector that is placed at the end of the procedure.

The callee, before exiting, executes code at the end to restore the registers.

(4) Caller saves callee's registers:

The caller executes a save/restore instruction that uses a bit/byte-vector found at the beginning of the code for the procedure body before and after the call. The registers are saved in the caller's activation record.

(5) Callee saves all registers: Described in the text.

(6) Caller saves all registers:

A save/restore registers utility routine is called before and after the call. The registers are saved in the caller's activation record.

12. The example illustrating label parameters in Section 13.5 assumes that static chains are being used for referencing nonlocal environments. Thus only a static link is necessary to describe an environment. Explain what is necessary to describe an environment if displays are being used instead of static chains. Redo the example assuming use of displays.

Ans: When displays are used, the environment at any point in an activation is defined by the values of all the display registers for that activation. When a label is bound as an actual parameter, the values of the display registers at the point of definition of the label can be passed as part of the parameter value. When a **goto** is executed the display registers are reset to the values sent in.

If the label is defined in the same block as the point of binding, then the current values of the display registers can be passed. However, the label may have been defined in some statically enclosing scope and one or more of the display registers used in the activation of that block may have been saved in the intervening activation records. To obtain the required values one must then follow the dynamic chain restoring the saved values of the display registers until the activation record of the block in which the label is defined is reached.

For uniformity, one can just pass the dynamic chain pointer for the activation that contains the definition of the label along with the location in code defined by the label. When a **goto** is executed, the dynamic chain is followed and the saved displays restored until the activation record pointed to by the parameter value is reached.

13. Explain in detail what computation is done to implement each reference to the call-by-name parameter J of **procedure** P in the first example in Section 13.6.

Ans: Each reference to the parameter J results in a call to the *thunk*, that implements the parameter, to provide the *l-value* of the parameter. The *thunk* computes the address of A(I), where I is bound to the declaration in the outer block.

6.12. Chapter 14 Solutions

5.   Analytically or empirically determine the magnitude of the space savings available through use of syntax tree implementation optimizations discussed in Section 14.2.3, such as subtree sharing and trivial node removal.

Ans: Trivial node removal can change the asymptotic complexity. But so long as all interior nodes in the syntax tree have at least two children, the size of a tree is linear in the number of its leaves, which is the size of the program.

It is possible for subtree sharing to change the asymptotic complexity, but it would have to take place above the level of leaves. In fact, to realize a more than linear reduction in space, there can be no bound on the height of the shared nodes in the tree. The reason for this is that if all sharing were restricted to occur below some level in the tree lying only a constant number of levels, c, above the leaves, the portion of the tree lying above that level is about $\frac{1}{2^c}$ times the size of the whole tree. Since c is a constant, that is a linear function of the original size.

6.13. Chapter 15 Solutions

1.   Assume we are generating code for the BB1 architecture of Section 15.4.3, and have three registers
     available for use as operand registers. What code would you generate for the following code frag-
     ment assuming all variables are statically allocated integers or arrays of integers?

Ans:

```
C       := 1;
A       := B–C*D;
D       := C + B;
X(B)    := C;
X(A)    := X(A) + X(D+1);
```

```
(1)     (LOAD, #1,t1)        — # denotes immediate operand.
(2)     (LOAD, D,t2)
(3)     (*, t1,t2)
(4)     (LOAD, B,t3)
(5)     (–, t2, t3)
(6)     (LOAD, B,t2)
(7)     (+, t1, t2)
(8)     (STORE, D,t2)
(9)     (LOAD, B,t2)
(10)    (STORE, X(t2),t1)
(11)    (LOAD, D,t2)
(12)    (+, #1,t2)
(13)    (LOAD, X(t2),t2)
(14)    (+, X(t3),t2)
(15)    (STORE, X(t3),t2)
(16)    (STORE, C,t1)
(17)    (STORE, A,t3)
```

The successor to the BB1 architecture is the BB2. The BB2 contains all instruction forms of the
BB1. It also includes a 3 register instruction of the form OP Reg1,Reg2,Reg3, where Reg3 :=
Reg2 OP Reg1. What BB2 code would you generate for the above code fragment?

Ans:

```
(1)  (LOAD, #1,t1)
(2)  (LOAD, D,t2)
(3)  (*, t2,t1,t3)
(4)  (LOAD, B,t2)
(5)  (−, t3,t2,t3)
(6)  (STORE, A,t3)
(7)  (+, t2,t1,t3)
(8)  (STORE, X(t2),t1)
(9)  (LOAD, A,t2)
(10) (STORE, D,t3)
(11) (+, #1,t3)
(12) (LOAD, X(t3),t3)
(13) (+, X(t2),t3)
(14) (STORE, X(t2),t3)
(15) (STORE, C,t1)
```

2. In some machine architectures, register allocation is complicated by the fact that use of a register R in an instruction implicitly includes another register R′. For example a multiplication involving R_i may store a double-length product in R_i and R_{i+1}. Alternatively, a three address instruction, OP Reg_i,Reg_j,Reg_k, can be "squeezed" into two address form by requiring that k=j+1.

How would you organize a GetReg routine for a machine that includes implicit register references? To make the problem more tangible, assume your GetReg routine will be used with a BB3 architecture. The BB3 is essentially the BB1 machine of Section 15.4.3 except for the fact that instructions of the form OP X,Reg_i, where X is either a register or storage address, store their result in Reg_{i+1} rather than Reg_i.

Illustrate your routine by generating BB3 code for the code fragment of exercise 1.

Ans: The GetReg routine must be extended to handle requests for two consecutive registers. In addition, the code generation routine may request a register consecutive to another allocated previously. This is to accommodate the case in which the allocation of a register to a variable or a temporary value occurs before the register is actually used in an OP instruction. The requests for single registers are handled as before. The extensions for the two cases are given below:

(i) Get two consecutive registers.

```
If there exists some register R with cost(R)+cost(R+1)=0 then
   choose R
else C := 2;
   loop
      If there exists at least one register R with
           cost(R)+cost(R+1) = C then
           choose that register R such that, the earliest next reference
           to any of the variables and temporaries associated with R and R+1
           is the most distant
           exit;
      end if;
      C := C+2;
   end loop;
   Save the value of R and R+1 for any associated variables or temporaries
   with a status = (L,S) or (D,S)
end if;
return R;
```

(ii) Free register R+1.

Note: If R+1 is not free, this routine will check to see if it is cheaper to copy R to another register R′ so that R′ and R′+1 can be used.

```
If cost(R+1)=0 then
   Reg := R
else C := 2;
   loop
      If cost(R+1)=C then
           Reg := R; exit
      elsif there exists at least one register R′ such that
           cost(R′)+cost(R′+1)+2 = C then
              — cheaper to free R′ and R′+1 and copy R to R′
         Reg := R′ such that the earliest next reference to any of the
                    variables or temporaries associated with R′ and R′+1
                    is the most distant
         exit;
      end if;
      C := C+2;
   end loop;
   If Reg is different from R then
      save the value of Reg for any associated variables or
      temporaries with status = (L,S) or (D,S);
      Copy R to Reg;
   end if;
   Save the value of Reg+1 for any associated variables or
   temporaries with status = (L,S) or (D,S);
end if;
return Reg;
```

The following code assumes that four registers are available for use as operand registers.

```
(1)  (LOAD, #1,t1)        — Single register allocation
(2)  (LOAD, D,t2)         — Double register allocation
(3)  (*, t1,t2)           — t3 contains C*D
(4)  (LOAD, B,t2)         — Single register allocation
                          — t3 can be reused to hold result
(5)  (–, t3,t2)           — t3 associated with A
(6)  (+, t2,t1)           — t2 associated with D
(7)  (LOAD, B,t4)         — Single register allocation
(8)  (STORE, X(t4),t1)
                          — Request made to free t3 to compute D+1
(9)  (STORE, A,t3)
(10) (+, #1,t2)           — t3 contains D+1
(11) (LOAD, A,t4)         — Single register allocation
(12) (STORE, D,t2)        — t2 freed with zero cost
(13) (LOAD, X(t3),t2)     — Single register allocation
                          — t3 can be reused to hold result
(14) (+, X(t4),t2)        — t3 associated with X(A)
(15) (STORE, X(t4),t3)
(16) (STORE, C,t1)
```

4. In Section 15.4.1 we noted that computations can sometimes be included as part of an address calculation. For example, IBM 360/370 machines include an addressing mode that that adds a pair of registers (one a base register, the other an index register) plus a constant displacement to form an address.

Show the tuples that would be generated for A(I) where A and I are local variables accessed via display registers. Outline how a code generator for these tuples might exploit the base-plus-index address mode described above.

Ans:

```
(1) Load  I,Reg1             — Address of I formed by adding a constant
                               offset to the display register
(2) Mult  #ElementSize,Reg1  — Omit if ElementSize = 1
```

The address of A(I) is

$$(BaseReg,Reg1,StartAdrOffset(A)-ConPart*ElementSize)$$

Sometimes addressing modes can be used to efficiently compute ordinary expressions. For example, consider A*B+C*D+1. First A*B and C*D are computed into (say) R1 and R2. The obvious next steps are to add R2 to R1, then add 1 to R1. A less obvious, but better, code sequence is to generate LA R1,1(R1,R2). This instruction uses the base-plus-index address mode to add R1+R2+1 in one step, storing the result in R1 (LA is a load address instruction).

How would you go about extending a code generator for + to produce this efficient, but non-obvious, code sequence?

Ans: The code generator can delay generating code for both address calculation as well as expression evaluation whenever addition is required. In expression evaluation, the code generator can represent addresses of temporary values as a tuple (t1,t2,c) with the understanding that the contents of the two addresses and the constant c will be added to provide the final value. The code generator for + can check the operands to determine whether an addition required to get the value of one of the operands could be combined with the current addition. If both the operands are already evaluated into temporaries, or one of the operands is a constant, no code is generated and the result is represented by the tuple.

In the example above, the code generator, when called for the first addition (A*B+C*D), will not generate any code. The value of the expression will be represented by (R1,R2,0). When called for the second addition, the value of the expression will be represented by (R1,R2,1). The load address instruction will be generated when the value of this expression is used.

6. Run-time checks are often required to verify that arrays, pointers, and constrained variables are used properly. If checking code is generated naively, the size and speed of a program can be significantly impaired.

For example, assume we have a tuple of the form (TestRng,I,L,U) that tests whether I is in the range L..U. This tuple can be used to check both subscripts and constrained variables. If $L \leq I \leq U$, (TestRng,I,L,U) has no effect; otherwise, a constraint exception is raised (probably leading to program termination). A naive code generator will generate a TestRng tuple before each subscript operation. In the example of exercise 5, assuming A and B are 10 by 10 arrays, this would produce:

```
(TestRng,I,1,10)
(Index,A,I,T1)
(TestRng,J,1,10)
(Index,T1,J,T2)
(TestRng,I,1,10)
(Index,A,I,T1)
(TestRng,J,1,10)
(Index,T1,J,T2)
(TestRng,I,1,10)
(Index,B,I,T3)
(TestRng,J,1,10)
(Index,T3,J,T4)
(/,T2↑,T4↑,T5)
(:=,T5,T2↑)

(+,I,1,T6)
(TestRng,T6,1,10)
(Index,B,T6,T7)
(+,J,1,T8)
(TestRng,T8,1,10)
(Index,T7,T8,T9)
(TestRng,I,1,10)
(Index,B,I,T3)
(+,J,1,T8)
(TestRng,T8,1,10)
(Index,T3,T8,T10)
(TestRng,I,1,10)
(Index,A,I,T1)
(TestRng,J,1,10)
(Index,T1,J,T2)
(*,T10↑,T2↑,T11)
(:=,T11,T9↑)
```

Extend the value-numbering techniques of Section 15.4.2 to identify and remove redundant TestRng tuples. Illustrate your extension on the above tuple sequence.

Ans: Every TestRng tuple is associated with a temporary name Ni such that the name corresponds uniquely with the operands. That is, if N1 and N2 are associated with the tuples (TestRng,I1,L1,U1) and (TestRng,I2,L2,U2) respectively and (I1=I2), (L1=L2), (U1=U2) then (N1=N2). Note that the names Ni do not correspond to any temporaries allocated for code generation. They are used for the redundant code elimination only. Every TestRng tuple is said to define the name associated with the tuple. Hence LastDef for these names correspond to the number of the last TestRng tuple that defined them. A (TestRng,I,L,U):N is redundant if

LastDef(I) < LastDef(N) **and** LastDef(L) < LastDef(N) **and** LastDef(U) < LastDef(N)

The numbering generated is given below:

Note: Only those columns that result in redundant tuples are shown.

			N1	N2	N4	$T1_a$	$T1_v$	$T2_a$	$T2_v$	$T3_a$	$T3_v$	T8
(1)	(TestRng,I,1,10):N1		1	0	0	0	0	0	0	0	0	0
(2)	(Index,A,I,T1)					2	2					
(3)	(TestRng,J,1,10):N2			3								
(4)	(Index,T1,J,T2)							4	4			
(5)	(TestRng,I,1,10):N1	R										
(6)	(Index,A,I,T1)	R										
(7)	(TestRng,J,1,10):N2	R										
(8)	(Index,T1,J,T2)	R										
(9)	(TestRng,I,1,10):N1	R					.					
(10)	(Index,B,I,T3)									10	10	
(11)	(TestRng,J,1,10):N2	R										
(12)	(Index,T3,J,T4)											
(13)	(/,T2↑,T4↑,T5)											
(14)	(:=,T5,T2↑)								14			
(15)	(+,I,1,T6)											
(16)	(TestRng,T6,1,10):N3											
(17)	(Index,B,T6,T7)											
(18)	(+,J,1,T8)											18
(19)	(TestRng,T8,1,10):N4				19							
(20)	(Index,T7,T8,T9)											
(21)	(TestRng,I,1,10):N1	R										
(22)	(Index,B,I,T3)	R										
(23)	(+,J,1,T8)	R										
(24)	(TestRng,T8,1,10):N4	R										
(25)	(Index,T3,T8,T10)											
(26)	(TestRng,I,1,10):N1	R										
(27)	(Index,A,I,T1)	R										
(28)	(TestRng,J,1,10):N2	R										
(29)	(Index,T1,J,T2)	R										
(30)	(*,T10↑,T2↑,T11)											
(31)	(:=,T11,T9↑)											

8. Redo Exercise 15.7, this time assuming a call to subprogram P has been added between statements 2 and 3. No knowledge of the registers used by P is assumed, so any registers whose contents are to be protected have to be saved before the call and restored after the call. However, if register associations are cleared before the call, unnecessary saves may be avoided.

Ans: Solution assuming four registers:

(1)	Load, B,t1
(2)	Load, C,t2
(3)	*, t2,t1
(4)	Load, D,t3
(5)	/, t1,t3
(6)	Load, B,t1
(7)	−, t2,t1
(8)	Load, D,t4
(9)	−, t1,t4

— Save registers before call and
— clear register associations

| (10) | Store, A,t3 |
| (11) | Store, D,t4 |

— Tuples required for the call to P

(N+1)	Load, A,t1
(N+2)	Load, C,t2
(N+3)	+, t2,t1
(N+4)	Load, D,t3
(N+5)	+, t3,t2
(N+6)	Store, A,t1
(N+7)	Store, C,t2

In the above solution, register 2 is not saved before the call even though it contains the value of C which is used later. Only the registers with status (L,S) or (D,S) are saved and the register associations cleared.

11.   In exercise 4 we saw that the addition of two registers and a constant could sometimes be performed in a single instruction if a base-plus-index address mode is available. Show how we can use peephole optimization to replace explicit register and constant additions with a single instruction that exploits a base-plus-index address mode.

Ans:

$$\text{Add Lit,R1; Add R2,R1; \%OpCode R1,\%ResultReg} \Rightarrow$$
$$\text{\%OpCode Lit(R1,R2),\%ResultReg}$$

Note that this rule can be used only if R1 is dead after the original sequence of instructions. Another rule should be added with Lit and R2 interchanged in the first two instructions.

14.   Show that RegisterNeeds, TreeCode and Commute each take time proportional to the number of operators in an expression tree to execute.

Ans: Each of these routines perform a depth-first search of the expression tree and the processing at each node is bounded by a constant. The number of nodes in a binary tree is bounded by $2*N+1$ where N is the number of operators(interior nodes) in the tree.

15. Sometimes the code generated for an expression can be improved if the associative property of certain operators (such as + and *) is exploited. For example if the following expression is translated using TreeCode 3 registers will be needed:

    (A+B) * (C+D) * ((E+F) / (G–H))

    Even if Commute is used, 3 registers are still required. However if the associativity of multiplication is exploited to evaluate multiplicands from right to left, then only 2 registers are needed. (First ((E+F) / (G–H)) is evaluated, then (C+D) * ((E+F) / (G–H)), finally (A+B) * (C+D) * ((E+F) / (G–H)).)

    Write a routine Associate that reorders the operands of associative operands to improve code quality.

Ans: Hint: Allow associative operators to have more than 2 operands. In RegisterNeeds, the register requirements of all the operands are considered. If all the operands require r registers, the operator requires r+1 registers. Otherwise, the operator requires the same number of registers as the most complex of the operands. Associate rearranges the operands in decreasing order of register needs.

18. The Schedule routine (Figure 15.23) heuristically tries to schedule left operands so that they are used after right operands, allowing them to be overwritten after their last use. As Figure 15.29 shows, this heuristic can fail. Outline how Schedule might be extended to properly handle shared sub-operands. Does your extension properly handle both dags in Figure 15.29?

Ans: Schedule always schedules the left subtree before the right subtree. A simple extension to cover the case in Figure 15.29 is to have one level lookahead for shared operands. If many nodes share an operand, the one which uses the operand as the left operand is always scheduled before any that use the operand as the right operand.

19. Explain how the code generation algorithms of Section 15.7 might be extended to handle the case in which commutative operators appear in a dag. Your extension should be able to interchange left and right operands of a commutative operator if this leads to better code.

Ans: The following code is inserted in the Schedule routine after the current node D has been scheduled:

```
if LeftOperand(D) is the right operand of another node
   scheduled earlier than D then
   if D is a commutative operator then
      if the RightOperand(D) is not the right operand of any node
         scheduled earlier than D then
         Interchange(LeftOperand(D),RightOperand((D))
```

23. Extend the Graham-Glanville code templates of Figure 15.38 to include templates that describe the following instructions:

- An addition of zero to any operand yields that operand without generating any code.

Ans:

> R1 —→   + 0 R1   {}

- Multiplication of a register by 2 can be implemented as an addition of that register with itself.

Ans:

> R1 —→   * 2 R1   {Add R1, R1}

- A three-address add instruction of the form Add Op1,Op2,Op3. This is defined as Op3 := Op1+Op2. The three operands may all be registers, or any one of the operands may be a direct or indexed address (with the other two operands required to be registers).

Ans:

R3 —→	+ R1 R2	{Add R1,R2,R3}
R3 —→	+ M R2	{Add M,R2,R3}
R3 —→	+ R1 M	{Add R1,M,R3}
R3 —→	+ ↑ + Const R1 R2	{Add Const(R1),R2,R3}
R3 —→	+ ↑ + Const R2	{Add Const(R1),R2,R3}
R3 —→	+ R1 ↑ + Const R2	{Add R1,Const(R2),R3}
R3 —→	+ R1 ↑ + R2 Const	{Add R1,Const(R2),R3}
Null —→	:= M + R1 R2	{Add R1,R2,M}
Null —→	:= + Const R3 + R1 R2	{Add R1,R2,Const(R3)}
Null —→	:= + R3 Const + R1 R2	{Add R1,R2,Const(R3)}

24. Assume we are designing a machine that will have two address instructions. The machine will have N operation codes and A addressing modes. Estimate the number of Graham-Glanville code templates needed to describe this machine.

Ans: The templates for the addressing modes can be factored out and used for both the addresses. There will be one template for each operation code and several templates for each addressing mode. The number of templates for each addressing mode depends on the the addressing mode and is usually small (permutations of operands, trivial and special operands etc.). The total number of templates required is then N + c*A, where c is a small constant.

Most real machines are not orthogonal. That is, not all combinations of addressing modes can be used with all operation codes. Does the set of Graham-Glanville code templates needed to describe a machine get bigger or smaller when non-orthogonal instructions are introduced? Can you give an upper bound (in terms of N and A) on the number of templates that may be required?

Ans: The number of templates increases for non-orthogonal instructions since the addresses can no longer be factored out of the templates for the various operation codes. For each operation code, templates must be provided for each combination of addressing modes. The number of templates required is then bounded by N*A*A for two address instructions.

26. Create attributed code templates, as in Section 15.8.2, that define the following instructions:

- Multiplication of an operand by a constant that is equal to 2^N, $1 \le N \le Max$, implemented by an arithmetic left shift of N bits.

Ans:

$$\text{Long(R)} \longrightarrow * \text{Const(C) Long(R) PowerofTwo?(C) \#GetPower(C,N)}$$
$$\text{InRange?(1,Max,N) \#Emit(ShiftL N,R)}$$

- Addition of a constant C, $1 \le C \le M$ to any register other than R0, realized as LA C(R),R.

Ans:

$$\text{Long(R)} \longrightarrow + \text{Const(C) Long(R) RegNotR0?(R) InRange?(1,M,C)}$$
$$\text{\#Emit(LA C(R),R)}$$

- Multiplications of the form Mult Opnd,R_i that require that i be even numbered and R_{i+1} be unused (since the product is formed in R_i and R_{i+1}).

Ans:

$$\text{Long(R')} \longrightarrow * \text{Long(O) Long(R) EvenReg?(R) \#GetNextReg(R,R')}$$
$$\text{Unused?(R') \#Emit(Mult O,R)}$$

Additional templates similar to the above but with the operand positions interchanged should also be created.

27. Using the notation of Section 15.8.3, an unconditional branch instruction is defined as:

    B Lab   PC $\longleftarrow$ Lab

where PC is the program counter. Explain how a peephole optimizer can discover, using this definition, that an unconditional branch to another unconditional branch can be collapsed into a single unconditional branch.

How is this optimization complicated if addresses used in branch instructions are not absolute but rather are relative to the current PC value?

Ans: Unconditional branch instructions are paired with the target instruction. Thus we have:

         B L1
    L1: B L2

This expands to

         PC $\longleftarrow$ L1
    L1: PC $\longleftarrow$ L2

Since the second instruction resets the value of PC without any intervening instructions in the execution flow, the first assignment can be replaced with the second. Note that the second assignment can be ignored only if there is no other instruction that references the label L1. Thus we get

```
            PC ← L2
      L1:   PC ← L2
```

This is matched by

```
            B L2
      L1:   B L2
```

If the addresses are relative to the current PC value then the value assigned to the PC at L1 depends on the PC value at L1. Hence, the right hand side of the assignment in the first instruction cannot just be replaced with the right hand side at L1. If the offset of L1 with respect to the first instruction can be calculated, then the address at the first instruction can be replaced with the sum of the address at L1 and the offset of L1 relative to the first instruction. However note that further optimizations may invalidate the computation of the offset of L1 relative to the first instruction.

28. After a peephole optimization is performed, the optimized instruction that is substituted for the original instructions is reconsidered and may be part of another peephole optimization. Give examples of cases in which peephole optimizations may be profitably cascaded.

Ans: Consider the following code that may be output for the translation of A(2*I):

```
      (1)   Load I,R1
      (2)   Mult #2,R1
      (3)   Subtract #4,R1
      (4)   Load 10(R1),R1
```

Instruction 2 can be replaced by an **Add** instruction while instructions 3 and 4 can be combined resulting in:

```
      (1)   Load I,R1
      (2)   Add R1,R1
      (3)   Load 6(R1),R1
```

If a base-plus-index address mode is available, instructions 2 and 3 can be combined resulting in:

```
      (1)   Load I,R1
      (2)   Load 6(R1,R1),R1
```

6.14. Chapter 16 Solutions

6. Show that the static activation record allocation technique of Section 16.2.2 always uses the minimum possible space assuming that all calling sequences shown in a call graph are possible.

Ans: Simply observe that there is a calling sequence that causes all the space allocated to activation records to be in active use at a single execution point.

7. Consider the program of Exercise 4. Assume that the program has been translated, but registers have not yet been allocated. The following table shows the number of registers needed by each routine:

Routine	Registers Needed
Main	3
A	1
B	2
C	1
D	3
E	2

Assume 8 hardware registers are available for allocation. How would you allocate these 8 registers to the main program and the subprograms so as to minimize register saves and restores across calls?

Ans:

Routine	Registers Allocated
Main	1 – 3
A	4
B	5 – 6
C	8
D	5 – 7
E	8 and 1

8. It is well-known that the problem of deciding whether an arbitrary program that does no I/O ever halts is undecidable. That is, no algorithm that correctly decides program termination in all cases can ever be created. Show that the halting problem can be reduced to the reachability problem. That is, if it could always be determined whether or not a given statement in a program was reachable during execution, then the halting problem could be defined in terms of reachability and solved. Because we know the halting problem cannot be solved, we may therefore conclude that the reachability problem must also be undecidable.

Ans: Add a new statement to the end of the program. Ask "is the new statement reachable?" If the answer is yes, the program halts. If the answer is no, the program does not halt. So the halting problem can be reduced to the reachability problem: if we can solve reachability, we can solve the halting problem.

9.   Explain how inline expansion of the following procedure call would be performed. What optimizations are made possible by the inline expansion?

```
A : Real := 2;
B : Real := 21;

procedure P(Flag : in Boolean; S : in out Real) is
begin
    if Flag then
        S := S **2;
    else S := S/A;
    end if;
end P;

P(False,B);
Write(B);
```

Ans: Dead code elimination, constant propagation, constant folding.

12.   We noted that recursive calls can cause problems if they appear within a subprogram that is expanded inline. It is clear that in some cases such recursive calls can be tolerated. For example, if Fact is a factorial function, implemented in the usual recursive manner, a call Fact(5) can readily be expanded inline, and the expansion may be optimized to a single constant value.

Can recursive calls whose arguments are constants always be safely expanded inline? In not, what further restrictions are needed to control inline expansions that involve recursion?

Ans: Recursive calls with constant arguments certainly *cannot* always be expanded inline, because such calls are not guaranteed to make a finite number of recursive calls. In the case of Fact(5) we know there will be a small number of recursive activations of Fact. From a theoretical point of view, we cannot always determine automatically whether or not the expansion process would terminate. This problem is undecidable, since we can easily take an instance of the halting problem (some program whose termination is in question) and transform it into an instance of this problem. Just take as a constant argument some representation of the program whose termination properties you want to know, and pass the program to a procedure that simulates the program by calling itself recursively and executing one instruction each time it is activated. This recursive procedure will expand forever if and only if the original program does not terminate. So in general the question "will this inline expansion terminate?" is undecidable, just like the question "will this program terminate?"

From a practical point of view, we must be satisfied with expanding only cases where we can be sure the expansion process will terminate. In other words, when in doubt, we will not expand. We establish some sufficient condition to guarantee expansion termination. For example, we might require that (1) only one parameter of the recursive call differ from its value in the parent activation, (2) that parameter be of type integer, and (3) the values of that parameter, in successive calls, form an arithmetic sequence that reaches the parameter value defining the base case of the recursion.

Theoretically, there is no end to the effort we could expend trying to find more cases that can be expanded. But practically, we will reach a point of diminishing returns fairly quickly.

14. Calls to a function are easier to optimize if it is known that the function has no side-effects. Ada and Ada/CS allow only **in** parameters, so actual parameters cannot be changed during a function call. However, variables may be changed during a call and this sometimes leads to side-effects. Assume the Def set of a call to a function is computed. Explain how this set may be used to decide if the call causes side-effects.

Ans: Recall that, if F is a function, Def(F) contains the variables that are changed directly by the statements of F. For F to be side-effect free, it is necessary that Def(F) not contain any variables that are global to F. But a call to F can change other variables, besides those in Def(F), via the calls made within the body of F. To be sure F has no side effects, we must be sure none of the routines that F can invoke, directly or indirectly, can introduce side effects to F. To check this, we must compute Def(G) for all G reachable from F, and take the union. If that union contains no variable that is global to F, then F is side-effect free.

Note that it is not necessary for all G reachable from F be restricted to having only **in** parameters. However, if G calls H and H has an **out** parameter, then the actual parameters corresponding to the **out** formals must be included in Def(G).

The discussion above is sufficient if routines cannot have *own variables,* that is, local variables whose value persist between calls. Own variables are not generally global to F, yet they constitute a part of the program state and changing their values can affect subsequent execution behavior when a routine in which they are visible is called again. To correctly handle programs with own variables, we should again construct the union of all the Def(G) sets for each G reachable from F, but now we check whether the union contains any variables that are (1) global to F or (2) own variables. If the answer is yes, we must presume F can cause side effects. If the answer is no, we can be certain that it does not.

15. Show that the ComputeUseSet algorithm of Figure 16.7 always terminates. Next show that the Use sets it computes are exact. That is, if a variable v is used during a call to P then v∈ Use(P) and if v∈ Use(P) then v actually may be used during a call to P.

Ans: It terminates because Use sets only grow during the computation, they never shrink, and there are only finitely many variables.

Exactness can be proven by induction on the shortest call path. Assume all control paths are possible. That is, presume both branches of all conditionals are taken.

17. In Section 16.3.1 we noted that factoring loop-invariant expressions from **while loop**s is unsafe, even if the expressions are very busy. The reason for this is that **while loop**s may iterate zero times, and in general it is impossible to predict in advance whether the Boolean expression that controls the loop will initially be true. On the other hand, Pascal's **repeat-until** loop allows loop-invariant very busy expressions to be safely factored, because it must iterate at least once.

Show that a **while loop** can be rewritten into a **repeat-until** loop entered through an **if** statement. Explain how this transform can be used to safely factor loop-invariant very busy expressions in **while loop**s. Under what circumstances is this transformation undesirable?

Ans: The transformation is undesirable if the loop is rarely entered or tends to iterates only a few times before exiting. In that case the transformation enlarges the code size but rarely improves execution speed.

22. Assume we wish to create a program LiveSubprogramVariables(P) that identifies variables that are live upon entrance to subprogram P. When compiling a call to P, LiveSubprogramVariables(P) could be used to determine what variables must be saved prior P's execution. We have already studied live variable analysis, but LiveSubprogramVariables(P) suggests an additional concern — how to handle subprogram calls that appear in P. Because of possible recursion, insertion of a subprogram's data flow graph at the point of call is infeasible.

As an alternate, design an iterative approach. Let LiveSubprogramVariables(P,1) be a first approximation to LiveSubprogramVariables(P) that assumes all variables are live on entrance to P. To compute LiveSubprogramVariables(P,2) use LiveSubprogramVariables(Q,1) to characterize the effect of a call to Q in P. Similarly, to compute LiveSubprogramVariables(P,i) use LiveSubprogramVariables(Q,i−1) to characterize the effect of a call to Q in P. Continue until LiveSubprogramVariables(P,i) = LiveSubprogramVariables(P,i+1).

Show that this iterative approach terminates and that at termination

   LiveSubprogramVariables(P,i) = LiveSubprogramVariables(P).

Ans: For the purpose of this analysis it is convenient to think of calls as dividing basic blocks into smaller blocks: one small block before the call, one after the call and one small block consisting of the call itself. We can still use the same data-flow equation:

$$LiveIn(b) = LiveUse(b) \cup (LiveOut(b) - Def(b)), \text{ where}$$
$$LiveOut(b) = \bigcup_{i \in succ(b)} LiveIn(i),$$

except we have to say what $LiveUse(b)$ and $Def(b)$ mean when b is a call to a procedure P. Recall $LiveUse(b)$ contains the variables that are used without first being defined in b. So, if b is a call to P, then $LiveUse(b) = LiveIn(b_P)$, where b_P is the first block of P.

Similarly, $Def(b)$ contains variables that are always defined in b without an prior use. Calculating $Def(b)$ is a simple matter of inspection for blocks without calls. But calculating $Def(b)$ where b consists of a call is a global data-flow problem. $Def(b)$ contains all the variables that are defined on all paths through P and are defined before being used in P. Since P may make calls to other procedures, we naturally consider an iterative solution.

The iterative approach generally collects path characteristics at each block, and this is convenient for us, even though we are really only interested in the characteristics of paths that start at procedure entry points. To help us compute $Def(b)$ where b is composed of a call to P we collect $KillIn(b)$ and $KillOut(b)$, for all $b \in P$, where $KillIn(b)$ and $KillOut(b)$ are defined by the following system of equations.

$$KillIn(b) = Def(b) \cup (KillOut(b) - LiveUse(b)), \text{ where}$$
$$KillOut(b) = \bigcap_{i \in succ(b)} KillIn(i).$$

(We define initial blocks of procedures to have no predecessor, and exit blocks to have no successors. An empty union is the empty set.) Intuitively, $v \in KillIn(b)$ if all paths starting with b reach a definition of v and that definition comes before any use. Now we can define $Def(b)$ where b consists of a call to P by $Def(b) = KillIn(b_P)$.

So $LiveUse(b)$ and $Def(b)$ have to be computed iteratively for blocks consisting of a procedure call. Notice that the equations defining $KillIn(b)$ use $LiveUse(b)$, which is an alias for $LiveIn(b_P)$ when b consists of $call(P)$, and the equations defining $LiveIn(b)$ depend on $Def(b)$, which is an alias for $KillIn(b_P)$ when b consists of $call(P)$. This is situation is not surprising because it is clear that the variables that are used before being defined in a procedure, P, may depend on which variables are defined by the calls made within P, and vice versa. Hence, an iterative solution will compute $KillIn$ and $LiveIn$ sets simultaneously.

Notice that calculating $KillIn(b)$ is an all-paths problem, whereas calculating $LiveIn(b)$ is an any-path problem. Consequently we must initialize these two groups differently.

```
    for each b∈ B loop
      KillIn₀(b)=B
      LiveIn₀(b)=φ
    end loop

    j := 0

    repeat
      for each b∈ B loop
        LiveOutⱼ(b)=    ⋃    LiveInⱼ(i)
                      i∈ succ(b)
        KillOutⱼ(b)=    ⋂    KillInⱼ(i)
                      i∈ succ(b)
      end loop

      j := j + 1

      for each b∈ B loop
        If b consists of call(P) where b_P is the first block of P then
          LiveInⱼ(b):=LiveInⱼ₋₁(b_P) ⋃ (LiveOutⱼ₋₁(b) – KillInⱼ₋₁(b_P))
          KillInⱼ(b):=KillInⱼ₋₁(b_P) ⋃ (KillOutⱼ₋₁(b) – LiveInⱼ₋₁(b_P))
        else
          LiveInⱼ(b):=LiveUse(b) ⋃ (LiveOutⱼ₋₁(b) – Def(b))
          KillInⱼ(b):=Def(b) ⋃ (KillOutⱼ₋₁(b) – LiveUse(b))
        end if
      end loop
    until (∀b,LiveInⱼ(b) = LiveInⱼ₋₁(b) and KillInⱼ(b) = KillInⱼ₋₁(b))
```

Each iteration of the **repeat**-loop applies one function to $KillIn_j$ and $LiveIn_j$ to get $KillIn_{j+1}$ and one to get $LiveIn_{j+1}$. We call these functions $Kill(LiveIn,KillIn)$ and $Live(LiveIn,KillIn)$. Kill is monotone in its second argument and anti-monotone in its first. (Anti-monotone means $L_1 \subseteq L_2 \longrightarrow Kill(L_1,KillIn) \supseteq Kill(L_2,KillIn)$.) Similarly, Live is monotone in its first argument and anti-monotone in its second. Thus the program defines a sequence of pairs under the recurrence

$$(LiveIn_{j+1},KillIn_{j+1})=(Live(LiveIn_j,KillIn_j),Kill(LiveIn_j,KillIn_j)).$$

The LiveIn components increase and the KillIn components decrease. Since there is a finite number of blocks and variables, the sequence must converge and the algorithm terminate.

We must show that this algorithm computes correct $LiveIn(b_P)$ sets for each procedure P. This proof has two parts: (1) variables that are live on entry to P are in $LiveIn(b_P)$; (2) variables that occur in $LiveIn(b_P)$ are live on entry to P.

Proposition (2) can be shown by induction on j, the number of the iteration in which v is added to $LiveIn_j(b_P)$. It is necessary to show simultaneously that a variable, v, that does not occur in $KillIn_j(b_P)$ is not always defined by P before being used.

For proposition (1) we can show that a variable v that is live at the entry of P will appear in $LiveIn(b_P)$ by using induction on the number of our smaller blocks between b_P and the reaching use of v. It is necessary to simultaneously (in the same induction) show that a variable w that is not defined by all paths through P or that is not always defined before a use of w in P will be removed from KillIn(b_P).

These proofs illustrate the common technique of proving inductively an proposition that is stronger than the theorem one really wants. In this case, the theorem we want only talks about LiveIn. But to show that LiveIn is computed correctly at each step, it is necessary to show that KillIn is also computed correctly. In particular, to show the induction step for proposition (1), we need to know that KillIn$_j$(b) does not contain variables having uses j blocks away in order to show that LiveIn$_{j+1}$(d) does contain variables having uses j+1 blocks away. Similarly, in the step for (2), we need to be able to use the fact that variables that have been removed from KillIn$_j$(b) should have been.

24. Recall that a dominator of a basic block b is any basic block d such that all paths to b must pass through d. One crude way to compute Dom(b), the dominator set of b, is to list all acyclic paths from the initial block, b_0, to b. The set Dom(b) is exactly the set of nodes that appear in all the acyclic paths listed.

A neater approach is the following. By definition, Dom(b_0) = {b_0}. Approximate Dom(b), b ≠ b_0, as B, the set of all basic blocks. This approximation is clearly an overestimate. Now observe that for any basic block b, Dom(b) = {b} $\cup \bigcap_{i \in P(b)}$ Dom(i). That is, b always dominates itself. Moreover, if c dominates B, it must also dominate all of b's immediate predecessors.

Create an iterative algorithm that computes dominator sets for all basic blocks using the approach outlined above. Show that the dominator sets that are computed are correct.

Ans:

```
for each basic block b∈ B loop
    Dom₀(b) := B
end loop;
Dom(b₀) := {b₀}

j := 0

repeat
    for each basic block b∈ B loop
        Dom_{j+1}(b) := {b} ∪  ⋂  Dom_j(i)
                             i∈P(b)
    end loop
    j := j + 1
until ∀b,Dom_j(b)=Dom_{j-1}(b)

for each basic block b∈ B loop
    Dom (b) := Dom_j(b)
end loop
```

First we check that the program terminates. The first key observation is that Dom$_{j+1}$(b)={b}$\cup \bigcap_{i \in P(b)}$ Dom$_j$(i) is a monotonic function of the Dom$_j$(i)'s. (Recall, a function f is monotonic if $x \subseteq y \Rightarrow f(x) \subseteq f(y)$.) Each time the **for**-loop is executed, it applies a monotonic function to the vector of Dom sets.

The second key is that the set of basic blocks in the program, B, is finite. $Dom_0(b)$ is initialized to B. In each successive iteration, $Dom_j(b)$ must either get smaller or stay the same. To check that claim, note that in the first iteration the sets certainly cannot get any larger. So we have $\forall b, Dom_1(b) \subseteq Dom_0(b)$. If we apply the body of the **for**-loop to each of these vectors, Dom_0 and Dom_1, the results must bare the same order as the the original values. Thus, $\forall b\, Dom_2(b) \subseteq Dom_1(b)$. Intuitively, it is clear this idea can be repeated indefinitely, and, naturally, it can be made formal by using induction on j to show that for each j, $Dom_{j+1}(b) \subseteq Dom_j(b)$. Since the $Dom_j(b)$'s only get smaller, there is a bounded number of iterations that can occur before none of the Dom(b)'s change. Once we reach a j where $Dom_j(b) = Dom_{j+1}(b)$ for all $b \in B$, the algorithm halts. The sequence has converged to a fixpoint.

Next, we show that if $d \in Dom(b)$ then all paths to b pass through d. To show this, we prove the contrapositive: if some path to b does not pass through d then $d \notin Dom(b)$, using induction on the length of the path from b_0 to b that does not pass through d.

Basis: Suppose there is a path of length zero from b_0 to b not passing through d. In this case, $b = b_0$. So, $Dom_0(b_0) = \{b_0\}$, and $d \notin Dom_0(b_0)$. Since $P(b_0) = \phi$, applying the body of the **for**-loop does not change the value of $Dom_j(b_0)$. Hence, $\forall j > 0$, $d \notin Dom_j(b)$, implying $d \notin Dom(b)$.

Step: Assume that if b' can be reached from b_0 without passing through d by following a path of length n then $d \notin Dom(b')$. We show that if a block b that be reached from b_0 without passing through d by following a path of length n+1 then $d \notin Dom(b)$.

Consider such a block b. Let i be a block that precedes b (i.e., $i \in P(b)$) along a path of length n from b_0 that does not pass through d. By the induction assumption, $d \notin Dom(i)$. Consider the iteration on which d is removed from Dom(i). In the following iteration d will be removed from Dom(b) by the program. Since Dom sets only get smaller as execution proceeds, we have that $d \notin Dom(b)$ as calculated by the program.

The last thing we must show is that if $d \notin Dom(b)$ then some path that reaches b must not pass through d. This proof can be done by induction on the number of the iteration in which d is removed from Dom(b).

25.   Assume that dominators are computed as outlined in Exercise 24. Show that for each dominator set Dom(b), there is a unique member $i \in Dom(b) - \{b\}$ that is an *immediate dominator* of b. That is, for all $j \in Dom(b) - \{b\}$, $j \in Dom(i)$. If block i is immediate dominator of block b then i is the "closest" dominator to b and hence the most reasonable place to move code factored from b.

Ans: It is useful the think of $i \in Dom(j)$ as a less-than relation. In those terms, we want to show there is a least "proper" dominator of b. To do this we show that $i \in Dom(j)$ is a total order on $Dom(b)$. Since $Dom(b)$ is finite, this will imply that there is a least element.

All elements of $Dom(b)$ are comparable: for all $i,j \in Dom(b)$, $i \in Dom(j)$ or $j \in Dom(i)$. If some paths went through i first and others through j first, we could put together a path reaching b that would miss one of them, which is a contradiction.

The relation is reflexive: $i \in Dom(i)$ holds for all i. That's part of the definition.

The relation is anti-symmetric: $i \in Dom(j)$ and $j \in Dom(i)$ implies $i = j$. To see this, imagine that all paths reaching j have passed through i and vice versa. We assume i and j are reachable, so the only way this can be is to have $i = j$.

The relation is transitive: $i \in Dom(j)$ and $j \in Dom(k)$ implies $i \in Dom(k)$. This just expresses the obvious intuition that if all paths to j have passed through i and all paths to k have passed though j, then all paths to k have passed through i.

This shows the relation defined by $i \in Dom(j)$ is a total order on $Dom(b)$, concluding the proof.

27.   Show that for any-path problems the algorithm of Figure 16.31 computes a minimal solution. That is, if $\hat{In}$ is any valid solution to the data flow equations, and In is the solution computed by the algorithm of Figure 16.31 then $In \subseteq \hat{In}$.
Hint — initially $In_0 \subseteq \hat{In}$.

Ans: In any-path problems we initialize $In_0(b)$ as the empty set. Therefore $In_0 \subseteq \hat{In}$. (Recall that In_0 is the vector of $In_0(b)$ values for all blocks b and the subset notation denotes the pointwise subset relation between components.) We now show that $In_j \subseteq \hat{In} \Longrightarrow In_{j+1} \subseteq \hat{In}$. That will complete the induction on j, proving $\forall j, In_j \subseteq \hat{In}$. Since $In = In_j$ for sufficiently large j, it will follow that $In \subseteq \hat{In}$.

Each iteration of the **repeat**-loop applys a monotonic function to In_j to get In_{j+1}. We know this because F_b is required to be monotonic for each b, because $\bigcup_{j \in P(b)} Out_i(j)$ is a monotonic function of Out_i, and because vector functions that are pointwise monotonic are themselves monotonic. We denote that monotonic function by $R(In_j)$ yielding $In_{j+1} = R(In_j)$. Also, since $\hat{In}$ is a solution to the data flow equations, $\hat{In} = R(\hat{In})$.

From $In_j \subseteq \hat{In}$ we must show $In_{j+1} \subseteq \hat{In}$. By monotonicity we have that $R(In_j) \subseteq R(\hat{In})$. But $In_{j+1} = R(In_j) \subseteq R(\hat{In}) = \hat{In}$. So $In_{j+1} \subseteq \hat{In}$.

6.15. Chapter 17 Solutions

1. Consider the following sparse array:

	A				B
C					
	D	E		F	
			G		
				H	I
	J		K		

Show how this array would be represented using the compressed rows technique and the double offset technique.

Ans: Using the compressed rows technique

V table:

Offset	0	1	2	3	4	5	6	7	8	9	10
Value	2:A	6:B	1:C	2:D	3:E	5:F	4:G	5:H	6:I	2:J	4:K

Row table:

Row No.	1	2	3	4	5	6
Offset	0	2	3	6	7	9

Using the double-offset technique

V table:

Offset	0	1	2	3	4	5	6	7	8	9	10	11
Value	1:A	2:C	3:D	3:E	1:B	3:F	4:G	5:H	5:I	6:J		6:K

Row table:

Row No.	1	2	3	4	5	6
Offset	−2	0	0	2	2	7

2. The array compaction utility discussed in Appendix F uses a best-fit decreasing approach to build a double offset array representation. That is, rows are meshed together in order of decreasing density. Moreover, when a row is meshed into the V table, the row is placed so that the V table is extended as little as possible.

Suggest an alternative to best-fit decreasing in selecting the order in which rows are meshed to form a double offset array representation. Under what circumstances will your alternative be superior to best-fit decreasing?

Ans: One plausible alternative is to use a different metric for measuring the "density" of the rows. That is, we still use best-fit decreasing approach, but instead of counting the number of nondefault entries in a row as the measure of its density, we take the widest "gap" in a row, where a gap is a number of "consecutive" default entries, as the measure of its density.

For example, the row

A		B			C	

has a widest gap of two entries, whereas the row

A				B	

has a (widest) gap of three (entries).

This approach may be superior under the circumstances where many of the less dense rows are sparse in gaps but not necessarily in nondefault entries. This situation has been observed in real cases. At least one result showed that "decreasing gaps" was better than "decreasing entries" for some LL parse table, but the opposite was true for a scanner table. Since table compaction is usually done only once, it really makes sense to try a few possible alternatives and choose the best one for that particular case.

3.   In some cases an array will contain two or more rows that are identical. Explain how the table compaction techniques of Section 17.1 can be extended to exploit identical rows in a sparse array.

Ans: There is a simple and effective extension to the compressed rows technique that takes advantage of identical rows. We just make identical rows share the same entries in the V table, i.e. identical rows will have the same offset in the row table. In this way, if we have n identical rows each has m entries, we only need m entries in the V table instead of $n \times m$ entries. The size of the raw table is the same though.

For the double-offset technique, it may seem harder and less effective to exploit identical rows in a sparse array. However, here is a somewhat trickier extension that one might want to try:

In the row table, each entry is flagged by one bit (or by using positive/negative numbers) which says whether the entry contains an offset to the V table directly or a row number to be used as the *canonical* row number to look up indirectly for its offset in the V table. All identical rows share the same entries in the V table, and they all use the same row number (their canonical row number), either directly or indirectly, to find out their offset value. The row numbers kept with the V table entries must also be the canonical row numbers.

For example, suppose rows 10, 14, and 25 are identical. We use the first row number, i.e. row 10, as their canonical row number. Now in the row table, the entry for row 10 contains the true offset to their entries in the V table, and the entries for row 14 and 25 will contain some encoding of the message: "go use row 10 for looking up entries."

Using this extension, we get a very slight increase (or none at all, depending on how entry values are encoded) in the size of the row table, there are no redundancies for identical rows in the V table, and the only overhead is one extra indirection at look up for some identical rows.

4. **if-then** and **if-then-else** statements in Pascal are typically generated by productions of the following form:

<stmt list> ⟶ <stmt>
<stmt list> ⟶ <stmt list> ; <stmt>
<stmt>   ⟶ **if** <expr> **then** <stmt>
<stmt>   ⟶ **if** <expr> **then** <stmt> **else** <stmt>

A common syntax error in Pascal is the "; **else**" problem — a ';' is immediately followed by an **else**. This error is surprisingly difficult to repair. The obvious solution is to ignore a ';' if it is immediately followed by an **else**. However in a one-pass Pascal compiler, parsing a ';' after a **then**-part will cause recognition of an **if-then** statement, with the **else** appearing to be the beginning of a new statement.

Add error productions to the above grammar so that a ';' **else** sequence is treated as equivalent to an **else**. Be sure that the updated grammar is still LALR(1).

Ans: The grammar given above is *not* LALR(1) because its ambiguity in handling dangling **else**s. We first transform them into equivalent LALR(1) productions:

<stmt list>   ⟶ <stmt>
<stmt list>   ⟶ <stmt list> ; <stmt>
<stmt>   ⟶ <open stmt>
<stmt>   ⟶ <closed stmt>
<open stmt>   ⟶ **if** <expr> **then** <stmt>
<open stmt>   ⟶ **if** <expr> **then** <closed stmt> **else** <open stmt>
<closed stmt> ⟶ **if** <expr> **then** <closed stmt> **else** <closed stmt>

Now we would like to add the error productions

<else> ⟶ ; **else**
<else> ⟶ **else**

with <else> substituted for **else** in the above productions. However, these error productions introduced a shift-reduce conflict in the context

with a lookahead of ";". (<closed stmt> can be reduced to <stmt> or ";" can be read as part of "; **else**"). This problem can be solved by changing the above grammar so that ";" is included on the right hand side of various productions generating statements:

<stmt list>	→	<stmt>
<stmt list>	→	<stmt list ;> <stmt>
<stmt list ;>	→	<stmt ;>
<stmt list ;>	→	<stme list ;> <stmt ;>
<stmt ;>	→	<open stmt ;>
<stmt ;>	→	<closed stmt> ;
<open stmt;>	→	**if** <expr> **then** <stmt ;>
<open stmt;>	→	**if** <expr> **then** <closed stmt> <else> <open stmt ;>
<stmt>	→	<open stmt>
<stmt>	→	<closed stmt>
<open stmt>	→	**if** <expr> **then** <stmt>
<open stmt>	→	**if** <expr> **then** <closed stmt> <else> <open stmt>
<closed stmt>	→	**if** <expr> **then** <closed stmt> <else> <closed stmt>
<else>	→	**else**
<else>	→	**; else**

Now in

... **if** <expr> **then** <closed stmt> ; **else** ...

we read the ";" then use lookahead to decide whether ";" is part of "<closed stmt> ;" or part of "; **else**". The error productions are vital in forcing the use of lookahead at this point.

5. Add Check_Input calls to the Micro parsing procedures of Section 2.4. Show how the following syntax errors would be handled:

  begin Id := 1 **end** $

Ans: A semicolon (;) is effectively inserted before **end** by the Match call in procedure Statement.

  begin Id := **end** $

Ans: Check_Input in procedure Expression would detect an error when it sees **end**, since **end** is most likely in the HeaderSet, it would simply signal the error and return.

  begin   **end** $

Ans: Since Check_Input in procedure StatementList would see the **end** instead of any valid first symbol, it would signal the error and return.

                $

Ans: The Check_Input call in procedure Program could not see any valid symbol, it would signal the error and return.

7(a). Give an algorithm that uses a CFG and a vector of insertion costs to compute the S table of Section 17.2.4.

Hint — Use an iterative algorithm that examines the right-hand side of each production.

Ans: The following algorithm computes the table of least-cost strings, S(A), where $A \in V_n$. It simultaneously computes C(A), iterating over the grammar until the costs converge to a minimum.

```
     — On input:
     —   For all a∈ Vₜ, a value C(a) ≥ 0 is provided, and all A∈ Vₙ, C(A) = ∞.
     —   For all a∈ Vₜ, S(a) = a
     — On output:
     —   Both C and S are correct up for all A∈ Vₙ
     procedure Compute_S(C : in out array [1 .. |V|] of Cost;
                 S : in out array [1 .. |V|] of TerminalString) is
       NoChange : Boolean;
     begin
       loop
            NoChange := True;
            for all productions p = (A —> X₁ · · · Xₙ) loop
               — remember that C(λ) = 0, and C(a), a∈ Vₜ, are given
               if C(X₁ · · · Xₙ) < C(A) then  — find one with less cost
                  C(A) := C(X₁ · · · Xₙ);
                  S(A) := S(X₁ · · · Xₙ);
                  NoChange := False;
               end if;
            end loop;
            exit when NoChange;
       end loop;
     end Compute_S;
```

7(b). Generalize the algorithm you defined in part (a) to compute E table values.

Ans: The algorithm to compute the E table is very similar in structure to the above algorithm.

```
procedure Compute_E(C : in array [1 .. IVI] of Cost;
            S : in array [1 .. IVI] of TerminalString;
            E : out array [1 .. IVI, 1 .. IVₜI] of TerminalStringOr?) is
    NoChange : Boolean;
    k : Cost;
    j : Integer;
begin
    — initialize E table
    for all X∈ V, all a∈ Vₜ loop
        E(X,a) := ?;
    end loop;
    for all a∈ Vₜ loop
        E(a,a) := λ;
    end loop;

    — main loop
    loop
        NoChange := True;
        for all a∈ Vₜ loop
            for all p = (A —> X₁ · · · Xₙ) loop
                let k := min(C(X₁ · · · Xᵢ₋₁) + C(E(Xᵢ, a)));
                        1≤i≤n
                if k < C(E(A,a)) then
                    let j be such that k = C(X₁ · · · Xⱼ₋₁) + C(E(Xⱼ, a));
                    E(A,a) := S(X₁ · · · Xⱼ₋₁) & E(Xⱼ, a);
                    NoChange := False;
                end if;
            end loop;  — inner for loop
        end loop;   — outer for loop
        exit when NoChange;
    end loop;
end Compute_E;
```

13. Show that the continuations computed by GetContinuation of Figure 17.28 are not always least-cost.

Ans: Following is a grammar which demonstrates that the continuations computed by GetContinuation are not always least cost.

```
S   —> T
S   —> U
T   —> λ
T   —> ( T )
U   —> ( U
U   —> ]
```

That is, the strings generated by the grammar are either of the form ((...()...)) or of the form ((...].

Let's suppose the insertion costs for "(" and ")" are both 1, and the cost for inserting a "]" is 5. Now, the continuations computed by GetContinuation for the parse stack after reading input ((... will always be a matching number of right parentheses ...)). For input strings of more than 5 left parentheses, the computed continuations certainly cost higher than using a single "]" as their continuations.

14. Validation of error repairs can be improved if semantic as well as syntactic validity is checked. Outline how semantic routines can be designed so that they can either screen error repairs or do full semantic processing.

Ans: We can make a uniform interface to all semantic routines such that:

(1) They all return a Boolean result indicating if any error was detected during the semantic processing.

(2) A switch, say CheckOnly, is used by all semantic routines to control their proper actions. If the flag is set, that means the compiler is in the "check only" mode, and no irreversible semantic actions, such as code generation or symbol table updates, should be performed.

With this interface set up properly, the validation parser can simply turn on CheckOnly flag and simulate normal parsing process. Whenever it sees an action symbol, it will call the proper action routine and check the return value. If any of the action routines return false (or the parsing cannot go on), the validation parser will return false to invalidate the suggested error repair. When normal parsing is resumed, the flag CheckOnly is set off for full semantic processing.

15. The LL(1) buffering technique of Section 17.2.1 is designed to handle any LL(1) grammar. Often LL(1) grammars have the property that nonterminals that derive λ do so directly. That is, if $A \Rightarrow^* \lambda$, then $A \longrightarrow \lambda$. Outline a simpler way of undoing parser actions for illegal lookaheads if all λ derivation is direct.

Ans: If all λ derivation is direct in the given LL(1) grammar, we do not need the buffer stack to undo parser actions for illegal lookaheads. Instead, we could effectively avoid any false prediction of λ productions by dynamically validating the lookahead symbols. The following algorithm does the dynamic validation of an input symbol to see if it is in the *true* FollowSet of a λ deriving nonterminal:

```
— Let S be the parse stack, A be the top symbol on S, and
— a be the next input token.  Let T be the parse table.
— The prediction T(A,a) is A —> λ
function CanFollow(S : in ParseStack; a : TerminalSymbol) return Boolean is
    B : Symbol;
begin
    — Let S = S₁ · · · Sₙ, where A = S₁ is the top (nonterminal) symbol
    — which predicted the λ production
    for i in 2 .. n loop
        B := S(i);        — get parse stack symbols from top to bottom
        if B∈ Vₜ then
            if B = a then
                return True;    — a could be matched later
            else
                return False;   — a is an illegal lookahead under this context
            end if;
        else              — B is a nonterminal symbol
            if T(B,a) is not a λ production then
                return True;    — since there is no indirect λ derivation
            end if;
            — else it's another λ prediction,
            — go on to check for next stack symbol
        end if;
    end loop;
    return False;         — a can not be matched under current context
end CanFollow;
```

Note that even if the input symbol is validated as a legal lookahead, we cannot pop off the λ deriving symbols from the parse stack in function CanFollow because there may be some action symbols in those λ productions.

16. Assume we are parsing an input x. Design a version of FindInsert (Figure 17.11) for which $O(|x|)$ invocations need only $O(|x|)$ time, even when the parse stack depth reaches $O(|x|)$.

Ans: We notice that the heart of FindInsert is its stack search and this is done to decide which stack symbol will be used to generate the error symbol. Once this symbol is chosen (say X_i), the necessary correction is uniquely determined ($S(X_n \cdots X_{i+1})$ & $E(X_i, a)$). We may observe that if a given vocabulary symbol, Y, is to be used to derive the error symbol, then only the *uppermost* (i.e. first) occurrence of Y in the parse stack needs to be considered (deeper occurrences can't lead to cheaper corrections). Thus rather than search the entire parse stack (which can require $O(|x|)$ time), we need only consider the first occurrence (if any) of each vocabulary symbol in the stack. This can be readily done after a bit of processing (performed, e.g., after the first syntax error is discovered). Let

$$Top : V \longrightarrow \{1,...,n\} \cup \{Absent\}$$

be a function mapping vocabulary symbols to their uppermost (i.e., top) occurrence (if any) in the parse stack. Further, let each stack symbol, X_i, be labeled with an integer value $IC(i)$, the cumulative insertion cost of X_i and all symbols below it in the stack. That is $IC(i) = S(X_i \cdots X_1)$. (Assuming $IC(Absent) = \infty$). Then to determine a least-cost correction we need only find a symbol, Y, which minimizes:

$$\underset{Y \in V}{Min}(IC(n)-IC(Top(Y))+C(E(Y,a)))$$

Once Y is found, Top(Y) gives its location on the stack and this (as noted above) determines the entire least-cost correction. Because this correction can be done in bounded time per invocation of FindInsert, we can establish linearity for this extended algorithm. For a proof of this linearity property, see [Fischer, Milton, and Quiring 1980].

17.   Prove that the LL_Repair algorithm of Figure 17.15 computes locally optimal error repairs. That is, the insertion string y and the deletion count i that it computes satisfies:

$$\underset{0 \le i \le m}{Min} \ \underset{y \in V_t^*}{Min} \{D(b_1 \cdots b_i)+C(y) \,|\, xyb_{i+1} \cdots \in L(G)\}$$

where the input $= xb_1 \cdots b_m$.

Ans: Let us use the notation (d,y) to denote a possible repair action which deletes first d input symbols from the remaining input $b_1 \cdots b_m$ and then inserts string y before b_{d+1} such that $xyb_{d+1} \cdots \in L(G)$. For a pair (d,y) to be a valid correction, it must be the case that $y \neq ?$ and $0 \le d \le m$. Such valid corrections always exist, because at the worst we can delete all remaining input and then insert S(CurrentParseStack).

It follows immediately from the definitions of LL_Repair and FindInsert that any pair (d,y) returned by LL_Repair is a valid correction. We want to show that this repair action is locally optimal. First, we make the following observations:

(1) $D(b_1 \cdots b_i)$ is nondecreasing on b_i's, i.e. $D(b_1 \cdots b_{i+1}) \ge D(b_1 \cdots B_i)$ for all $i \ge 0$.

(2)   In the algorithm of Figure 17.15, the value of $C(Ins)+D(b(1 .. d))$ can only decrease (from the **if** statement in the **for** loop).

(3)   FindInsert will always return a locally optimal insertion string for a given parser state and input symbol.

Now, consider other possible valid corrections (d′, y′) under the same parse stack and input symbol, there are three possible cases:

(a) $d′ = d$
Since we know FindInsert always returns locally optimal y, we know that CostOf(d, y) $\le$ CostOf(d, y′) for all other possible y′.

(b) $d′ < d$
This means we have already considered (d′, y′) in LL_Repair's **for** loop, and CostOf(d, y) $<$ CostOf(d′, y′) (from (2) above).

(c) $d′ > d$
From the loop exit condition of LL_Repair, we know that CostOf(d′, y′) $\ge D(b(1 .. d′)) \ge$ CostOf(d, y) (from (1) above and the fact that CostOf(d′, y′)

$= C(y') + D(b(1 .. d')) \geq D(b(1..d'))$ because $C(y') \geq 0$.

Since in all cases $Cost(d', y') \geq Cost(d, y)$, we conclude that LL_Repair computes locally optimal error repairs.

18.   When a syntax error is discovered, we normally do not undo parsing actions because semantic actions are difficult or impossible to undo. Since semantic actions are initiated by action symbols, undoing parsing actions up to the last action symbol processed should be feasible. This would allow a wider range of repair actions without requiring that semantic actions be undone. Outline how the standard LL(1) driver of Figure 5.11 can be revised so that when a syntax error is discovered, parsing is undone up to the last action symbol processed.

Ans: We can add a *buffer stack* for buffering parsing actions. Whenever a match or predict action is done, the associated terminal symbol or production is pushed onto the buffer stack. Whenever an action routine is called, the buffer stack is cleared. Then when a syntax error occurs, we could restore the parser to the state immediately after the last action symbol was processed. This is done by undoing the buffered parsing actions and put back the input tokens (which can be reproduced easily from the buffered actions). To undo a match, we push the terminal symbol onto the parse stack and put it back to the (front of the) input token stream. To undo a prediction, the right-hand side of the production predicted, which should be on top of the parse stack, is replaced by the corresponding left-hand side nonterminal symbol.

19.   Let a be some particular error symbol. Assume we wish to use the FindValidatedInsert routine of Figure 17.19, and that we have already computed the vectors $E(X,a,0)$, $E(X,a,1)$, ..., $E(X,a,i)$. Explain how to compute $E(X,a,i+1)$ using these vectors, the S table, and the grammar being parsed.

Ans: Following algorithm, which is similar to the one given in Exercise 7(b) for computing E table values, will compute $E(X,a,i+1)$ values.

— On input:
— E(X,a,0), E(X,a,1), ..., E(X,a,i) entries have been filled in.
— On output:
— E(X,a,i+1) values will have been filled in.
— Some properties that can be used to optimize this algorithm:
— (1) $C(E(X,a,i+1)) \geq C(E(X,a,i))$ for all $i \geq 0$
— (2) $C(S(X_1 \cdots X_{n+1})) \geq C(S(X_1 \cdots X_n))$ for all $n \geq 0$

```
procedure Compute_Ei(C : in array [1 .. |V|] of Cost;
             S : in array [1 .. |V|] of TerminalString;
             i : in Integer;
             E : in out array [1 .. |V|, 1 .. |Vt|, 0 .. N]
                   of TerminalStringOr?) is
   NoChange : Boolean;
   c : Cost;
   j,k : Integer;
begin
   — initialize E(X,a,i+1)
   for all X∈ V, all a∈ Vt loop
      E(X,a,i+1) := ?;
   end loop;


   — main loop
   loop
      NoChange := True;
      for all a∈ Vt loop
         for all p = (A —> X₁ ··· Xₙ loop
            if E(A,a,i) /= ? then   — otherwise E(A,a,i+1) is always ? too
               let c be    min      (C(X₁ ··· Xⱼ₋₁)+C(E(Xⱼ,a,k)))
                        1≤j≤n,1≤k≤i+1
               such that
               (1) c > C(E(A,a,i)), or
               (2) c = C(E(A,a,i)) and
                   if j, k are the values in the above formula that gives c,
                   then E(A,a,m) /= S(X₁ ··· Xⱼ₋₁) & E(Xⱼ,a,k)
                   for l ≤ m ≤ i, where C(E(A,a,l)) = ... = C(E(A,a,i)).
               — i.e. find the least-cost string that is more expensive than
               — the cost of E(A,a,i), or a "different" string that has the
               — same cost as E(A,a,i)
               if c < C(E(A,a,i+1)) then
                   let j, k be such values in the above formula for c;
                   E(A,a,i+1) := S(X₁ ··· Xⱼ₋₁) & E(Xⱼ,a,k);
                   NoChange := False;
               end if;
            end if;
         end loop;   — inner for loop
      end loop;    — outer for loop
      exit when NoChange;
   end loop;   — main loop
end Compute_Ei;
```